Made *for* You *and* Me

Me in our driveway, Gouldsboro, Maine, 1979.

Made *for* You *and* Me

GOING WEST, GOING BROKE, FINDING HOME

Caitlin Shetterly

voice

HYPERION / NEW YORK

Permissions, appearing on page 248, constitute a continuation of the copyright page.

Copyright © 2011 Caitlin Shetterly

Library of Congress Cataloging-in-Publication Data

Shetterly, Caitlin.
    Made for you and me : going West, going broke, finding home /
Caitlin Shetterly.
        p.   cm.
    ISBN 978-1-4013-4146-6
    1. Shetterly, Caitlin—Travel—United States.   2. Davis, Dan, 1979—
Travel—United States.   3. Married people—United States—Biography.
4. Self-employed—United States—Biography.   5. Unemployed—United States—
Biography.   6. United States—Economic conditions—2001–2009.   7. Blogs—Social
aspects—United States.   8. National Public Radio (U.S.)   I. Title.
    CT275.S4859A3 2010
    306.872—dc22

                                                            2010031229

Hyperion books are available for special promotions and premiums. For details contact the HarperCollins Special Markets Department in the New York office at 212-207-7528, fax 212-207-7222, or email spsales@harpercollins.com.

Book design by Jennifer Daddio / Bookmark Design & Media Inc.

FIRST EDITION

1   3   5   7   9   10   8   6   4   2

Dan

Women and children knew deep in themselves
that no misfortune was too great to bear if
their men were whole.

—JOHN STEINBECK, *THE GRAPES OF WRATH*

PROLOGUE

About a week after we got home it hit me, hard: "I'm almost thirty-five years old and I've just crossed close to four thousand miles of America in a hatchback with a two-month-old baby, a ninety-pound dog and my husband, Dan, to move in with my mother in Maine. My life as I knew it has officially collapsed and ended. I'm in some new zone: part limbo, part full-on life-altering change, part grace. And Dan and I are sleeping in separate beds."

It was this last thing that made me feel totally upside down. Somehow, two years earlier, when Dan and I got married, as if my independence had been magically erased, I became a person who has trouble sleeping if Dan's not in bed with me. I'm all too aware that his big lump of six feet and five inches of cozy flesh isn't a few inches away breathing, sometimes snoring, dreaming and twitching.

But in my mother's house, there simply wasn't a bed

comfortably big enough for both of us and our son safely in between. So I was sleeping in my childhood bed, which my mother had moved down to a small room off her living room. We call this room "the library," or sometimes "the Christmas room" because it's where we put our tree. Admittedly, "the library" sounds terribly grand; in reality, it's a small, bright room lined with simple wooden shelves filled with books and in one corner stands a desk that used to be Grammar's, my grandmother. It has a few comfortable cushions piled together on the floor and a cozy chair in another corner. Off the library is a tiny room, which we call "the back room," big enough for a single bed and a desk and above which my mother had a sleeping loft put in that fits one double mattress on its floor. Dan was sleeping in that loft. Although I missed Dan in the bed, our baby still needed me throughout the night to nurse. Giving up this mammalian bonding and putting him in a crib right then, when everything else about our lives was in such flux, felt like another big loss no one was up for. So, at night, in my childhood bed, with one eye open and one hand on his little body, I kept vigil to protect my son from our lives.

The worry wasn't that living with my mother this way would never end or that Dan and I would never be in the same bed again, although there were days when my skeptical optimism was certainly challenged. What this watchfulness meant and what kept me awake at night was that we were, in every way, a family trying to pull itself together, no matter how our basic survival needs might affect our lifestyle, personal dreams, or flimsy notions of what our lives *should* look like. I had no idea how long we'd be like this. From the distance of time I scoff a little at this anxiety because, truthfully, thank God we had somewhere to go—since the bottom fell out of the economy, many people have lost their homes or their spouses; some lost their lives. Families have had to hole up in motels or, worse, in cardboard shelters on the street. Still, for us, in our young marriage, in *our* story of *our* lives falling apart while we tried to do whatever it took to take care of our son, our dog and ourselves, we felt, essentially, flattened. Actually, it was worse than that: What we felt was that we could no longer dream. That was, possibly, the most dangerous aspect of what had happened to us.

Every night, Dan climbed the ladder to his perch, the mattress set on the floor underneath a skylight, and looked up through white pine branches to the stars and moon, and turned out the light. Every night, after I cocooned myself in bed next to my sleeping son's body and after our dog, Hopper, had climbed into the bed with me, I'd lie awake in the darkness. Not only was my mind bubbling with worry, but my body ached from being contorted into a snail shape around my son, my legs positioned diagonally across the mattress to give Hopper as much room as he needed. I used to carry with me a *New Yorker* cover from 2006, which I affixed to every fridge door in every apartment I ever lived in, of a blond man, who looked a lot like a cartoon depiction of John Updike, piled into a bed with his wife, children and cat. No one has any room in the drawing except the cat, who is sprawled out, the covers pulled up to its chin, taking up the whole bed while everyone else tries to accommodate it. This, in a nutshell, is how Dan and I have always slept with our animals and, now, our son. I can hear the hardliners already: We've inverted the natural hierarchy of the world. Or, worse, we're just plain nuts. Perhaps. But there must be something in it for us.

Honestly, at my mother's, I felt scared at night with Dan sleeping in the loft. That was the bigger thing—more than missing his body, per se—I was just plain frightened. He seemed miles away, which is part of the reason the dog was on the bed and I was holding on to my son (you might, then, ask the to-tally justifiable question: Who's protecting and parenting whom?). The library's double glass doors to the woods outside felt like a vulnerable porthole where anything or anyone could come in and hurt us. It seems almost silly to say that, since I grew up in these woods, in the boonies: I should have known better. What's there to be afraid of? Pine trees? The passing bears, coyote, bobcats, fishers, deer, fox, varying hares, bats and tree frogs? Truthfully, even with a pack of hungry coyotes, a starving bear and a bobcat gone mad, those woods are safer than most streets in Los Angeles. I knew this. My mother had taught me (nay, more like ingrained in me) a deep and passionate re-spect for the land and the animals we shared this piece of earth with. Because my mother was a wild bird rehabilitator when I was a child, on any given week, we had robins in our basement, a baby red-eyed vireo in our kitchen screaming for us to feed her, a saw-whet owl in the bathroom (not the most fun thing to encounter when you had to pee in the middle of the night), a raven named Chac who loved to steal my jewelry and suntan lotion while I was busy "lying out" on the lawn and listening to Casey Kasem's *American Top 40*, and an eider duck who hung out on our dining room table, reeking of fish. Because of my mother, I had raised three baby raccoons and, once, a baby skunk. These guests, although at times borderline humiliating to anyone who wanted to *keep* human friends, became our fam-ily. They also became part of the fabric that our family still weaves to tell our story to each other, to our friends and spouses, to our children.

Also, ever since my parents' divorce, my mother had made this small, protected piece of ground she lived on even more sacred. She had helped create a wildlife sanctuary in the acres surrounding the house, which protected the land from future development. Inside, she had rearranged the existing furniture and bought new furniture, giving away or tossing many of the objects of our past. Despite losing some of the stuff that signified our history, we gained my mother's cleaning out of her soul and mind to a point where she could make her own place in our family house. And she did all the things that somehow never got done with a marriage foundering, two kids, a dog, two cats, various wild animals and a couple of creative careers in one small house. For instance, she put doors that reached the floor on all the bedrooms—this may seem like an odd luxury, but when you've grown up in a house where your parents installed all these "beautiful" antique doors from yard sales and junk shops and then just affixed them—often with two-to-three-inch gaps at the bottom—when a new, solid, tight door gets put in, you feel like you've finally gotten a level of privacy fit for a king. A peaceful quiet had come over the house; it was now just a lovely home without the baggage of marital anguish. For all of these reasons, there was no reason not to feel emotionally or physically safe inside the house or outside, even in the pitch darkness.

I did, at least tangentially, know *real* danger in other places. Long before Dan and I went west, I taught acting for a time at a juvenile jail outside of Portland, Maine. What I saw there— from both the law-enforcement perspective and also the children's side—was that violence is so terrifyingly ingrained in our culture, it's no wonder some people feel that trying to fix anything or anyone with jail is a pointless Band-Aid for a much larger problem. Also, once, many years ago, while still living in Portland, I was followed home by a man who exposed himself and started masturbating on my front stoop while I somehow managed to get my key in the lock and myself through the door and then upstairs. And, later, I certainly wasn't safer from danger while living in L.A., which may be unrivaled in its glaring disparity between rich and poor and the violent tension that hovers in between. But here, home, I somehow felt more scared. My fear was something inside me, something existential that might not have been assuaged even *if* Dan had been able to fit in the bed.

Hopper was also scared of the dark. This was not very comforting. When I told Dan this, Dan told me I was crazy and that Hopper would rip anyone's head off who came near us. "Look at him," he'd say, and we'd both regard Hopper's enormous bulk of black and tan rottweiler-shepherd mix. But sometimes, when I took Hopper out for a late-night tinkle, we'd both stand on the porch, neither one of us interested in being the first to step off. He'd turn and look at me, his long Eeyore's face fairly confident I wasn't going to force him because then I, too, would need to get off the porch. I'd tell him, "Go on, Buddy. Go pee. I'm right here (ready to bolt, but nonetheless). Go on, Bud!" We'd stand like this for a moment and then, without even discussing it, we'd both turn back, no peeing having taken place. Neither one of us had stepped off into the dark and onto the damp, early spring ground that smelled so pungently of loamy earth and ice thawing, it made my mouth water. Neither one had disrupted the perfect orbs of light from the house which illuminated the first brave tendrils of grass coming up, feathery and emerald green. As soon as our backs were turned, we'd run the ten feet to the door like we were freaking Orpheus. I'd slam the door behind us and then we'd both be so relieved.

Some nights I'd find myself at four thirty a.m. standing at the bottom of the ladder to the loft where Dan was sleeping. I'd call up to him, "Dan, are you sleeping?" Silence. Of course he's sleeping, because he's willing to accept for the moment where our lives are and do what any sane person would do: get some rest so he can tackle all of it tomorrow.

I'd call him again. "Dan?"

Then I'd hear, muffled, like from underneath ten comforters, "No . . . ? What's wrong?" Whenever he says "no" like that, I know he's definitely been sleeping but that he's hoping that I'll think he was awake, too, working on figuring out whatever I'm awake mulling over, even though he was blissfully, irritatingly, asleep while I was doing all the mental gymnastics.

"I can't sleep. Our lives are chaos. And I hate this. I mean, I hate our lives being like this. I hate not sleeping in the same bed. I hate that nothing is solid and the only place we have that's ours is our car, which isn't even ours, it belongs to Toyota. And I feel overwhelmed and hysterical."

"Do you want to come cuddle?"

Pause. "No." I'm too wired for cuddling. Plus, cuddling seems like a hop, skip and a jump away from something else.

Always forgiving, always optimistic, my husband decides to ignore the sting of my "no" for the moment and focus on the hysteria at the bottom of the ladder. "Cait, I don't know what to tell you. It will get better. It has to."

In the half-light I look at the pile of bills that came across the country with us and still hasn't been opened. They're looming on my brother's dresser, which we've set up in this room for our clothes. Its three drawers are ornamented with a butterfly, a dragonfly and a ladybug my father painted when my brother was born—all of which are so picture perfect and beautiful they should be in National Geographic. "Someday," I think, "someday, our baby will have his own room, his own bed, his own dresser with paintings like that on it." But that day feels so far away, I almost can't bear it.

I want to scream, "How did we get here? Where did we go wrong?"

Instead, I say, "OK." And I go back to my bed and curl around my son, his little body safe as houses next to me. He reaches out his tiny hand and smiles in his sleep. I take it, and, like this, I fall asleep.

I

I got California on my mind
I'm leavin' this old town behind...

—"CALIFORNIA ON MY MIND,"
MERLE HAGGARD & THE STRANGERS

CHAPTER I

My new husband was packing and unpacking all of our belongings onto a dirty snowbank. It was the 30th of March, 2008, and unseasonably cold. Even though the sun was brilliantly shining, the temperature hovered around thirty degrees before windchill. From behind our living room window I could hear Dan swearing a blue streak. For two hours I'd been watching him reach in, shove things around inside the car, rip at our bags and throw them out onto the snow, then shove them in again. We were supposed to leave Portland, Maine, that afternoon for a weeklong drive across the country to start a new life in Los Angeles. Dan and four of his friends had already spent over three hours in the wind trying to negotiate our Thule bin onto the top of our car. A few days before, the movers had started out ahead of us with a truck full of our belongings. Now the things we'd earmarked to go with us in our car would not cooperate. There was no room for all our stuff; us; our dog, Hopper; and our cat, Ellison. Something, or someone, was going to have to go. Dan kept coming into our empty apartment to warm up his hands. Every time he came in, I'd say, "Hey, Dan, this isn't working. Maybe we need to rethink, sleep on this and leave tomorrow?" I was starting to get that kind of anxious that makes me freeze in one place and become totally useless. I was supposed to be packing the bathroom, but all I could do was watch my husband and freak out.

"No, Cait, we're going today," he responded. And then he went back outside to yank everything out of the car again and line it all up on the dirty snowbank. I had washed everything and neatly folded and packed it so that we could start out brand new and clean in our new life. I had gone so far as to buy two beautiful boat bags from L.L. Bean, one for each animal's gear. I had wanted to get them monogrammed with their respective names in big embroidered block letters, but Dan said that was a ridiculous waste of money. Looking outside at our duffel bags, CD cases, boat bags, one lone sleeping bag, pillows and books all strewn this way and that, I wasn't sure anything we had amounted to much. And, suddenly, I had no idea why we were leaving everything and everyone we knew.

Dan unpacked the car again and brought the bags and pillows, CD books and CDs all back inside and told me I needed to start throwing stuff out. When he gets like this I call him Deputy Dan. Because he's generally mild-mannered and mostly kind, when he's on a tear, I do what he says. I figure he's taking charge because we're in a crisis and this is what men do; they manage crises. Our friends Molly, Brian and Joelle had come over to say goodbye. They were starting to look a little nervous because, I'm sure, this whole thing seemed more disorganized and more wrenchingly unpleasant than anyone wanted to be party to. I was unclear about what things I was supposed to be tossing, exactly. I had just given most of our lives away to the church ladies down the street, including Dan's only pair of gloves, which could have been warming his hands right then. Meanwhile, thirty-five boxes of books, a bed, a bunch of wedding presents in the form of china and kitchenware, all of our dishes, an IKEA mattress, a Little Debbie rack we'd found outside of a burned-out convenience store and a couple of bookcases were all being shipped across the country by movers for close to three grand. Three grand was more than all of it was worth. Based on what I saw of the guys who packed our boxes onto the eighteen-wheeler, I wouldn't have been surprised to find out they were also running drugs. I was convinced I'd never see any of our things again.

"Uh, what stuff are you suggesting?"

"All that stuff you're packing in the bathroom—all that perfume you hardly ever wear. This pillow, this hat, this bag, these books, half of your clothes. They won't fit. We'll get this stuff again."

"But—"

"Cait. I'm serious. In a couple of months we'll buy all this shit, new. Nicer. Trust me."

"Are you sure?"

"It won't fit. I'm sure." He had a firm but slightly pleading look on his face that was hard to ignore.

I turned to Molly and said, "Hey, want these perfumes?" (One of which was a Christmas gift I had bought for myself when I was eighteen and living in Paris.) I was reluctant to actually hand the perfume to her and, as stupid as this is, I started crying about it. She was standing there like a deer caught in headlights, unsure as I described how wonderful my perfume was, if she should want it or not want it given she was Dan's friend as well. Instead I started trying to make my cosmetics bag thinner. I pulled out some nail polish and a few cotton balls. Deputy Dan was watching this parsimonious gesture. He walked past me into the bathroom, where I'd been trying all afternoon to concentrate enough to sort and pack our toiletries, and, in one swipe, took out a whole shelf of stuff with what seemed like the longest arm I'd ever seen and then dumped it all into a trash bag.

"We can get all that crap again." Then into the pile went the straw cowboy hat he got in Texas one spring break from college, a sweater, a few books and some jeans. Joelle put her head down and started helping me sort through our bags like she knew now was not the time to start arguing with Dan. Of course not, because he was acting like a maniac.

Dan pulled out my wedding dress and said, "This is not something you need right now." Yeah, no kidding.

Molly rushed in and said, "I'll hold on to it for you." I handed it over, even though I wanted it to go with us. Dan and I had only been married a few months, and this wedding dress—in which I looked, I will brag, fabulous—seemed like the most important material object to tether me to the lives we were leaving and also the future unfolding in front of us. Molly was getting married in six months and was starting to look for her own dress. Something in me started to worry that she might steal my dress and my whole wedding, even. Let's face it, she already had my perfume. Everything started to whirl around me like it does when a panic attack is starting. It was getting dark outside and I've always thought it's a terrible idea to start any trip in the dark. Morning is the time to leave places. Our wedding, just seven months earlier, flooded my boggled brain; my dress, his suit, the rain all morning clearing to the most beautiful puffy-white-clouds-against-a-blue-sky day, the wind. And I got this memory, as if I were behind a camera watching us that day: Dan and I are standing at the edge of a golden, undulating field. The bay by my mother's house is shimmering just over our shoulders, the pine trees bearing witness from the edges of the tall grass. Around us more than a hundred of our closest friends and relatives sit in the late-August light, their sun hats and dark glasses occluding their faces, their dresses and ties blowing in the wind. Dan, always a guy to stand on tradition, says his vows flawlessly. But when it comes time for me to repeat the richer or poorer line, I turn to my audience and say, "For what I hope will be richer!" and then mug for a laugh.

"OK," I thought. "This is what we're doing. We're doing the richer part. We're leaving Maine and moving to the land of milk and honey to make some money because my husband thinks this is the best thing we can do in an economy going south. He says we can replace all these things and he must be right. It's just stuff, anyway."

I let everyone else take over at that point because I was having trouble breathing. Before I knew it, I was sitting with three bags between my feet and Dan was shoving Hopper into the backseat on top of a pile of bags. I heard Brian say to Dan, "We can take Hopper if you don't have room for him" and Dan snapped, "No, he's fine," and then he slammed the door on Hoppy's tail. At this point the Deputy cracked and yelled,

"Fuck!" and opened the door to hold Hop, saying, "I'm so sorry, buddy." But this fissure in his armor was only momentary. A second later, he closed the door, this time with controlled gentleness, Hopper looking out at him, his face vulnerable. Ellison was as quiet as snow in the backseat. Deputy Dan turned, efficiently gave hugs to our friends, got in and started driving. Hopper was panting and tried to get from the backseat to the front to sit on my lap. The darkness fell like a pitch-black shroud around our tiny, rolling universe and I was crying my eyes out. "What are we doing?" I kept saying over and over and over again. What are we doing?

CHAPTER 2

When my parents, Susan Hand Shetterly and Robert Browne Shetterly Jr., moved to Maine in 1970, they were going back to the land. My father, a Harvard graduate, had handed over his draft card to William Sloane Coffin, the chaplain of Yale who was righteously opposed to the Vietnam War and supported young men who wanted to resist it. Dad had been arrested for protesting the war and had participated in the Harvard Strike of 1969. He and my mother, who had earned a master's of education from Harvard University, were pregnant with my brother, Aran. They wanted something else, something they could control from the earth up. The way they tell it, they were on their way to Canada, but Maine was too beautiful to not stop and so they ended up buying sixty acres on the coast in a town called Gouldsboro. The land was dense with both hard and soft wood, had a pond, a sand pit full of crickets and a small house on it, all for seven thousand dollars, their entire savings. They drove up their new driveway in a taupe-colored VW bus my paternal grandfather, Pop, had given them for a wedding present and started putting down roots, literally. They planted a garden, built a root cellar, got some chickens, erected an outhouse and bought a generator. They read everything about homesteading they could get their hands on and made a go of it.

In my memory, my parents were gorgeous people: My mother was thin and had long, honey-colored hair, bright blue eyes and a smile as big as the Atlantic Ocean. Some people said she looked like Jane Fonda and others, even more flatteringly, like Julie Christie. My father looked like a beat version of the young Marlon Brando with his dark hair and eyes and intense physical musculature. They were artists, but they weren't snobby, having been brought up to believe that they should give back rather than take. And they weren't into drugs. At all. Which always makes me laugh because in high school I asked my dad if he'd ever smoked pot and he told me he'd tried it twice but that it didn't do anything but give him a headache. Then he gave me a perplexed look as if to ask, "Is it just me?" There were people in Gouldsboro who surely thought my parents were educated but had no common sense to hole up in a house in the woods with no electricity, running water, or telephone and to try to grow everything they ate. But for others, I imagine, they were some kind of glamour couple, an example to be met and followed.

I don't know what my brother, Aran's, first four years were like as my parents tried gardening, killing chickens, digging ditches and clearing the land for firewood, but my guess is there were failures and successes, some bigger than others. By the time I came along, this was a life they were doing with perseverance and, also, some success. At least, the routine of it was becoming clear.

I remember our lives there as if we were living in some kind of Eden. And the truth of that and what we, as a family, eventually lost when we left there still aches like an old wound that never healed right. I have pictures of myself as a little girl picking vegetables in the garden or tapping trees for maple syrup with my father in the woods. I remember the path from the house to the garden, through a small grove of pine trees like I'm walking it right now: I can still taste the wintergreen that grew on its sides, smell the earthy white pine needles, feel the soft, giving ground underneath my feet. I can still remember with a heart's long clarity the winter nights, cold and dark, the yellow lights from the kerosene lamps and my father's deep voice as he sat by my bunk bed reading *Little House in the Big Woods* aloud to me, validating our lives with Laura's story. I loved it in Gouldsboro. What my parents built was magical.

But it was hard work. At the same time they were building this exceptional place in the world, doing it with a fervor as if they were specifically rejecting the war and the commercial trappings of our society with what they grew, what they ate and where they lived, they were teaching themselves to be artists. My father was learning to paint beautifully, in acrylics and oils, and also to draw animals and plants with precision. My mother was teaching herself everything she could about the natural world that surrounded her for essays she began publishing. And she was writing poetry. Their marriage was intense and hard. If you add all that together and then throw in two small children and inevitable financial strain, you have a potential time bomb. Eden, it turns out, is hard to sustain.

And so, when I was seven years old, we moved farther south down the coast to a small village. There our lives began to change. My parents built a house that had electricity, running water, a real toilet and private rooms for my brother and me. We were footsteps from the ocean. I was put, with help from my grandparents and a scholarship, in a private Waldorf School that, at that time, only went through the fourth grade. My brother started sixth grade at the local elementary. From a distance it might look like things were improving. Except they weren't. The problems in my parents' marriage followed them. I hated the school where I had to do everything, even math, with huge square crayons. The boys in the older grades started to tease and flirt with me, which made me intensely uncomfortable, as if the blankets had been pulled off while I was asleep. My brother became a stranger as he courageously went out into his new life playing sports, making friends and going to a different school. I know my parents thought they were giving Aran and me opportunities we couldn't have had in our old community. And they were right. The schools were better and the values of the teachers and the people around us seemed to mimic ours more closely. But it was as if our lives had been cauterized at a certain point and an expulsion had somehow taken place. We all grieved for what we had built in the woods just an hour away—so close it seemed like we could go back at any moment, except we couldn't.

It took twelve years for my parents to split up and divorce and for our lives to move on. We began trying to learn a new version of the word "family," something we pieced together as we grew and changed.

For most of my life I was haunted by this loss of perceived, complicated paradise. Something in me was always reaching home to Gouldsboro, comparing everything in my life and my choices to those my parents had made. After a gap year in Paris and my college years in Providence, I moved to New York City to be a writer and an actor. Both my brother and I always, for whatever reason, seemed to end up in cities, far away from our roots. I missed Maine, though, and felt, somehow, inferior to my parents for not being married and having children by my early twenties, for not raising a garden and making a sustainable life. It felt callous to be career-chasing, wearing all black and smoking Camel Lights. During summers in the city, I would lie in bed and miss Maine—not just Maine; I still, almost fifteen years later, missed Gouldsboro—so much it hurt.

But in the summer of 2001, I suddenly, unexpectedly, fell in love with New York City. This wasn't the same kind of soul-filling devotion I'd had for Gouldsboro or the heady love I'd felt for Paris, or even the ironic appreciation I'd had for the wackiness of Providence. I don't know what changed, except that it was one of the most beautiful summers in the city I'd ever known—cool and dry, deliciously empty. And something about my life felt settled in a way that I had hungered for. I was starting to make a home for myself, and my career was beginning to come together: My first book—a book of short stories I had collected and edited about divorce—was coming out that fall, on September 4. I was excited about the small tour the publisher had arranged and proud of the book. I had begun working freelance for public radio and had published a few pieces in some national women's magazines. I was studying acting and had directed a short play I'd written. In many ways my life was beginning to feel, to quote Walker Percy, "certified."

There were some problems, though. Ben, the man I was living with, was the kind of person you can never pin down; I was always hungry for more, always insecure. And I hated our dark apartment, which we never managed to make into a home together. I couldn't stand that he subsisted mainly on Coke, pizza, McDonald's, Cap'n Crunch and instant flavored oatmeal, whereas I worked at the farmer's market on the corner of Ninety-Seventh and Amsterdam, selling vegetables from an upstate farm (a whiff each week from whence I came) and brought home garbage bags full of veggies that I taught myself to cook in unexpected and wonderful ways. (The best way, I found, to make okra—something I had previously thought was a slimy, disgusting mess—was to wash it, slice it into thin rounds, throw it into a pan with some olive oil, a little sliced, fresh Serrano pepper, and some salt and then fry it until crispy. I like to serve okra this way with eggs in the morning or for dinner with a nice piece of flank steak seared in brown butter and a hunk of warm, crusty bread.) I spent many meals savoring my creations alone while Ben scarfed down two takeout slices from the Sal & Carmine's a few blocks up on Broadway and washed them down with a Nesquik chocolate milk. Even so, New York was opening up to me.

Then 9/11 happened and everything changed. I remember the blue blue sky, the still air, the roiling sense of panic turning into dread and then deep anguish. I remember looking at Ben, who wanted to stay in our Upper West Side apartment and "hold down the fort" while I wanted to go out and do something, anything, to help. And I realized, *This is over. I cannot stay with this person in this life.* It was like a page had been turned.

My book came out to little fanfare because, obviously, Americans were focused on our national tragedy. And, soon, we began a war in Afghanistan. Although more than 50 percent of us are divorced, war and fear, understandably, loom larger in the American psyche than anything else.

So, a long year later, in the fall of 2002, I called a writer friend of mine who spends some of his time on the coast of Maine and I said to him, "I think I'm done with this chapter of my life." He said, "Pack up and come home, Caitlin." So I did. I gathered up my cat Ellison, my laptop, a pair of boots and a down coat and came home to Maine for Thanksgiving. I never went back. In one fell swoop I knew that I was finished with my boyfriend and New York City. I needed a life that felt safer.

For a couple of weeks I surfed between my parents' houses, toting Ellison in a small plastic cage. Finally, I presented my father with what I figured was a totally reasonable plan: He would help me move to Rome, Italy. He looked a little shocked. So I suggested, as a fallback, Paris, France (this was, at least, familiar ground for me, and I could easily move there with my cat—no quarantines and she'd love French cheese!). He told me that in my fragile state he felt I should go no farther than Boston. So I moved three hours south to Portland because I could get a bigger bang for Daddy's buck; the apartments were large and cheap and I wanted, more than anything, space. I spent my first year detoxing—everything from cigarettes to my ex-boyfriend to the physical fear I'd been carrying around in my body since 9/11 seeped, slowly, out my pores. I threw myself into my work and filed more stories for public radio than ever before. I began a column for a local paper about love and relationships in a small town and I founded a nonprofit theater company, a dream I'd never had the gumption or the energy to fulfill in New York. I started loving being alone.

And then I met Dan.

Here's the thing: I really really didn't want to meet Dan. I was thirty and thin and boyfriendless and loving my life and my small, perfect apartment with a tiny office to write in and a huge view of all of downtown Portland, the harbor, out to the ocean and three lighthouses. I spent every evening doing yoga or writing.

But one Saturday night, the weekend before Thanksgiving, in the fall of 2004, at about ten thirty p.m., while I was in the midst of writing a column for that week, my doorbell rang. My friend Apple was standing there. She asked me out to a bar to meet another friend of hers, a guy photographer, up from Boston. I went, grumbling, because I really was having a very nice time by myself. However, I am preternaturally disposed to say "yes" when I mean "no," a problem that has gotten me in more scrapes than I'd like to admit, even to my therapist. I was still wearing an old black turtleneck sweater with a hole under the arm that I'd had for years, a pair of faded "misses" Levi's, and some Merrell sneakers I'd bought to go hiking in Baxter State Park that fall with my mother. I pulled on my ripped, white, fake fur jacket, which I'd purchased years before at the Salvation Army on Ninety-Sixth and Broadway and had named Marilyn for Marilyn Monroe. I threw my hair into a loose ponytail. There was a part of me that knew this was a possible set-up with Apple's unnamed "friend." But I wasn't interested. I was sure I could make that clear with my insouciant appearance. I may have deigned to put on some lipstick, but I don't think so.

When Dan walked in, I was sitting at the bar of Norm's Downtown Lounge on Congress Street, drinking a cosmopolitan. He was six foot five, blond, blue eyed and handsome in an all-American kind of way. The way he hugged himself, with his hands in the pockets of his black boiled-wool jacket, reminded me of Jon Voigt in *Midnight Cowboy*. I don't know why. He certainly doesn't *look* like Jon Voigt. But, maybe, it's because there's a searching, fragile quality to his aspect which I associate with that character. He was soft-spoken and there was a shy kindness about him and also a determined and firm morality that immediately tethered me. I took one look as Dan walked toward me, hand outstretched, and thought, "Shit."

When Dan first kissed me, he leaned into my car like some kind of Tom-Cruise-you-complete-me-maverick and took my whole face in his hands. I was stunned. Everything up till then had been very polite and chaste. I felt connected to him but unsure that I really wanted to get into all the messiness that joining your life with another person's entails. I liked the control of what I had: my Bikram yoga practice, my cat and my stock dinner of black beans simmered in olive oil with fresh farmer's market tomatoes, onion, garlic, hot cherry bomb peppers, a splash of balsamic vinegar and some salt and pepper, served with a baked potato and salad. My life was, like the twenty-six postures of Bikram, wonderfully predictable.

But Dan had gotten to me. That first night at Norm's he told me about a film he was obsessed with called *The Killer of*

Sheep, a black-and-white made by a guy named Charles Burnett about the isolation of poor blacks in America. Dan related to the desperation of poverty that stifles dreams. He said he knew firsthand what it was like to feel invisible. He spoke so eloquently and openly about both the film and his own experience growing up poor and white in a trailer park outside of Portland, I was stunned into paying attention, because most people weren't this honest or this real. I had been searching a long time for both honest and real. While he talked, I watched his very large, capable hands rest in front of him on the bar with a calm that was weighted by a bottle of beer. His face was open, but something also told me he had street smarts—a quality I've always lacked and respected. Late that night, after talking for hours and hours, our small group got up to leave Norm's. Dan held the door open for me as I pulled Marilyn around my shoulders. When we got to the street he stuck out his hand and gave mine a shake good night and then he and his friend Nicky took off into the darkness, Dan's six-five, hands-in-his-Levi's form walking a shortened gait to stay in step with Nicky's smaller, livelier, springy pace.

A few days later, just before Thanksgiving, I checked my e-mail at my mother's, where I'd gone for the long weekend. There was a note from Dan. It said simply: "I lost my cell phone on the bus back to Boston. I can't find Apple's phone number. Can you send it to me?" It didn't occur to me that this was ridiculously helpless because, clearly, if he had any brains he would call 411 or look it up in the phone book. So I wrote back. And then, about four days later, he wrote to thank me and to tell me he'd bought a new phone. He then asked me for *my* phone number. I gave it to him and he called the next day. We started having these wonderful conversations that were more like happenings than self-conscious "I want to sleep with you but am willing to jump through the conversation hoops to make you feel safe" calls. I'd get off the phone exhilarated by the discussions we were having about art and film, my brain whirring with ideas. I didn't feel pressured in any direction. There was no "Hey, want to go out on a date this week or next," or anything that came dangerously close to that. These conversations weren't building to an obvious crescendo. They were just wonderful moments.

Finally, he did ask me if I wanted to go out to dinner and we agreed I would come down to Boston, where he was living, just before Christmas and we'd have a meal and see a movie. Over saag paneer, chana masala, naan, and mango lassi at a small Indian storefront in Cambridge, we talked and talked and talked until the restaurant closed and then we went across the street to the coffee shop and talked some more. We never made it to the movie.

Dan drove back up to Portland with me—ostensibly to spend the night with friends, but he tells me now that he just wanted to spend more time gabbing in the car. Later, after all that conversation, which had made me hoarse (I was unused to talking that much to anyone!), he got out of the car and said good night. He didn't try anything. He just went off into the darkness. I drove home and lay down on my bed and realized I felt happy, relaxed and totally open to the world in a way I hadn't felt in a long time or, maybe, ever.

The next night Dan called and asked if I wanted to go out for a beer. It was then, at the end of that second night, after close to a month of phone calls and one dinner, that he kissed me.

I spent the better part of the next four months trying to lose him. I was scared of the commitment and I knew, intuitively, that if I was going to be stuck with this guy for what might end up being a long time, I should try to shake him first. Something adhered me to him in a way I'd never felt, and this frustrated me because I still harbored cowgirl fantasies from my childhood about going west, riding horses and becoming a cowboy's sweetheart. I still had some big, sunny dreams I wanted to chase. Also, I'd been burned enough in relationships, which, when combined with my fear of divorce, had made me exceedingly skittish. But he stayed right there, patiently.

Dan drove me crazy by doing things like taking all my laundry to the Laundromat and then coming home with some much heavier woman's clothes—sweatpants and enormous pairs of cotton granny underwear, none of which he'd ever seen me wear before. He lost things constantly (he once left our car keys in the sand at the beach, never to be recovered once the tide roared in as we swam), he couldn't hear me speak to him from the other room but could listen to a conversation three tables over in a noisy restaurant just fine, he suffered from male pattern refrigerator blindness, and he and his buddy Frank were always up to cockamamie shenanigans that involved repairing old cars and cameras to one day sell and, often, just breaking them more. But he tried hard and his heart was in the right place. Also, he was tolerant of me in a way that was either just plain stupid or saintly. He allowed me to write about our lives in my dating column, using, ironically, "cowboy" as his moniker because of a big belt buckle he wore (and still wears to this day) with a rooster on its face. He was supportive. He wasn't threatened by my career or goals. Instead, he was inspired. And he gave me lots of space in which to figure out how I felt.

When Dan asked me to marry him, he almost drove us off the road. We had been together for two years and were basically living in my place but, as a safety net (this was my idea), he still had his own apartment. We'd gone ahead and adopted Hopper together from The Animal Refuge League; we were already making a feline/canine/human family together. That Saturday night, after a lobster feast twenty-five minutes away at my dad's, we were driving home to my mother's little saltbox in the woods. We'd taken the animals up for the weekend to savor the last halcyon days of August and were indulging in everything from blueberry pie to ice cream to daylong swims in the ocean. Dan jerked the car to the side of the road with the erratic energy of John Cleese in a *Fawlty Towers* episode. He killed the engine in front of the long golden field by the bay where I grew up, opened the glove box, pulled out a ring and said, "Will you marry me?"

I had no idea this was coming. My first words were not the appropriate "Yes!" or even "Horrors, no!" but "You're so fucking stupid." I have no idea why I said that. But later he would jokingly tell me that he should have heeded those words. The next thing I said was "Yes." And I really meant it.

A year later we were married in that same field. Anyone who ever saw a photo or was there will tell you it was the most beautiful wedding, ever. We planned it and executed it ourselves. Our friend Joelle picked our flowers from roadsides and her parents' gardens, and Frank helped hang lights and build a bridge from the road to the field. We had a huge white tent, candles everywhere and the most gorgeous blueberry-vanilla-lemon cake covered with a shimmery, sugary fondant that was, in turn, covered with blue and yellow edible flowers. I still dream about how that cake tasted—like bottled sunshine and summer in Maine. We found every blue canning jar for flowers and every speckled enamel tub for lobster shells at yard sales and flea markets. Our steak came from a nearby farm, our seafood from local fishermen and our appetizers, salad and coleslaw all from the gardens of people we knew. Everything was homespun and gorgeous. We also wrote our own vows. Mine were funny and sharp with a little heartfelt thrown in. Dan's, on the other hand, were something out of a movie. He had remembered my telling him how much I loved that scene in Shakespeare's *Henry V*, when Henry asks Katherine to marry him. She can't really say no—he's just won her country and her hand—but nonetheless, for dramatic purposes, the scene is there. And it's funny and sweet, sexy and swooningly beautiful. I guess I always related to her because she was named "Kate" and, also, there was a part of me that didn't believe that a modern girl like me would ever get the chance to be wooed with such stalwart eloquence. In the middle of his vows (and I almost didn't get it at first) Dan started saying: *If thou would have such a one, take me; and take me, take a soldier; take a soldier, take a king.* My heart was putty.

Our first dance was to Tom Waits's "Long Way Home," which, I did not know at the time, would become the theme of the first few years of our marriage:

"I put food on the table/and a roof over our head/But I'd trade it all tomorrow for the highway instead/Watch your back/keep your eyes shut tight/your love's the only thing I've ever known/One thing's for sure pretty baby/I always take the long way home . . ."

I relive that day often and go back and back and back, wishing I could do it again and just be there once more to experience the food and the sunshine and my husband in his beautiful brown Italian wool suit and my gorgeous, flowing dress that was made of a material that crinkled all over with silvery threads, had a train that fanned out behind me like a mermaid's tail and was strapless. I'd had a shawl woven for me of ivory bamboo with the tiniest amount of gold thread running through the stitching that made it shimmer when I moved. I wore, at the V of my dress where my cleavage began, a round, golden starfish brooch covered with tiny white pearls, which my mother had worn at her wedding, her sister had worn at hers and, before that, my grandmother, Grammar.

But that's the problem with weddings: After all that work, they're just over too quickly. For our honeymoon we drove up to Prince Edward Island to camp. We spent our days swimming and, in the evenings, we ate mussels. We drove all over the island making photographs and super-8 movies until, finally, it began to rain, filling our tent with pools of standing water despite two tarps. The rain got to Dan, and late one night he decided that he must be allergic to mussels and was possibly dying from eating too many. I asked him a series of (what I thought were pertinent) questions about the level of pain and suffering he was enduring until he cried out that I wasn't "validating his feelings." "Welcome to marriage, folks," our friend Ken told us when we got home and told him our story.

Many things in our lives were perfect: We loved our animals, we loved each other, we loved much of the work we did and we loved our rented apartment. But there was this small corner of us, individually and together, that wanted more. For different reasons we were both people who had spent a good deal of time running from our lives. I wanted to run from the pain of my parents' ruptured marriage, and Dan wanted to get as far away from the trailer park as he could. With all of this running built into our DNA, neither of us enjoyed standing still for too long. And, also, our ambitions and dreams were always trained on what we thought might be greener pastures somewhere else, where we might be bigger players in more expansive markets. There was something, always, about Portland and Maine that felt too small somehow, like there was a glass ceiling that we were always banging our heads against. In the backs of our minds we just expected that someday—sooner rather than later—we'd try to live someplace else, somewhere that might give our careers the playing fields we craved.

But at that time, this desire was more like the intermittent drone of an elusive mosquito in a hot July bedroom. We didn't yet know how real it was about to become.

CHAPTER 3

I had always wanted to go west. Ever since my mother sang me to sleep with "Red River Valley," I wanted to be a cowboy, or, second best, a cowgirl. In my twenties, living in New York City, I would go home at night to my cat and small studio apartment and lie in the dark, imagining the adventures I could have if I pulled on a pair of cowboy boots, packed up a duffel bag and hit the road. I read Gretel Ehrlich and Pam Houston and, in the dark, alone, I thought that I could be as tough as they were, sleeping in the wide open, sometimes, even, in the snow. But life in New York City, so all-encompassing, was always getting in the way. Plus, I was chicken.

Until I met my husband.

Dan has a way of fixing his gaze on something and not letting go, as if Manifest Destiny is so ingrained in his personal road map that nothing can get in his way. Although he grew up with little, Dan wasn't going to let a lack of money hold him back. He put himself through school at the Maine College of Art by working as a bartender and snow plower. Sometimes he had to take time off until he'd saved enough money for the next semester. He'd walk into the bursar's office with a huge wad of cash held tight with a rubber band and hand it over. When he received his BFA in photography, he was the first person in his family to have attended and graduated from college.

When I married Dan, I knew I was marrying someone from a different background from mine. Mine is what my mother has always called "downwardly mobile with a vengeance." My parents came from privilege but went out on their own and worked extremely hard to create a homestead and a family. They made money to support us by digging clams, driving a scallop boat and cutting sardines in addition to their careers as artists. Dan came from hardworking folks who were, at times, painfully poor but were survivors. No matter what adversity was thrown in their way, they persevered. Dan and I had one major thing in common: We both knew how to work hard and hustle.

No matter what financial challenge was thrown in Dan's and my paths, we were always able to find a way through. I call Dan my "solutions guy" because he can figure out how to fix anything from a broken chair to an empty bank account. Sometimes that has meant Elmer's glue and sometimes it's meant selling our entire CD collection.

Dan's ability to believe in the proverbial green light was obviously what had gotten him out of the trailer park and into college and a career; he is stubborn in that kind, self-effacing way that salt-of-the-earth Mainers have. I'm a fighter, too, and can plow through most things, but there's always a moment when I think, "I can't" and get stuck. Maybe this is why I was never a great cross-country runner—I couldn't hold the finish line in my gaze long enough to make it matter. Dan, though, can make me keep going even when I don't want to. He'll pick up the slack, he'll tell me I can, he'll say, "Put your head down, grit your teeth and hold on." This can be totally maddening when I want to fold and say in as loud a voice as possible, "Attention, *people*, this ain't workin'!" but, also, it means that as a couple we get things done and don't get waylaid in my "I can'ts" for too long.

When the recession came home to us in December of 2007, I felt stuck and shocked. Dan's full-time job as a studio photographer had been changed to part-time. In those days I was running my theater company, working for public radio and taking the odd writing assignment, all of which, when combined with Dan's full-time $40,000 a year plus benefits salary, had been keeping us together. We didn't yet have the extra income we needed to start saving to buy a house and we couldn't go on vacations anywhere, but we paid all our bills on time, ate really well, had regular dinner parties, and went to the movies every other week. We had friends in L.A. who were making killings as photographers and working in the film business, and they had been beckoning us to sunnier skies, bigger dreams and larger paychecks for years. I had already filed one theater piece for NPR from Los Angeles and my producers wanted more. We figured, though, that with the incremental gains we were each having in our careers while living what was a very nice, quiet life in Maine, sooner or later we'd be able to buy a house there and start a family. But when the recession hit and Dan's company downshifted, taking away more than a third of his salary, we could no longer afford our apartment, even with the second job Dan had picked up as a weekend bouncer at a local bar. Dan looked at me one night over dinner and said, "Look, our lives are about to change drastically, no matter what we do. Let's go west. Let's go to L.A." Dan had gone west once before when he went to college in San Francisco. He'd only made it through one year before he'd had to come home. Even with his scholarships and loans, even with his job at Starbucks, he couldn't afford San Francisco prices enough to live and eat. He was constantly hungry and never had sufficient money for art supplies. So, he came home and started over. Since we'd been together we had visited L.A. a few times and had been romanced by the tall palm trees, the warm breezes, the healthy food and the beautiful people. Los Angeles seemed like a modern version of the Celtic legend of Tír na nÓg, the land of eternal youth and happiness our Irish ancestors believed in. And we've always loved movies and television. There's nothing like the thrill I get when I see an incredible performance in a film, like, say, Tommy Lee Jones's as a grieving, furious father searching for his son, dead or alive, in *In the Valley of Elah*. Or a visual moment, like the one in that wonderfully intense Danish movie *The Celebration* when the handheld camera jiggles up to the most unbelievable blue sky you've ever seen. I was romanced by the gritty, dissolute honesty of movies like *Laurel Canyon* and *Crash*. I looked across the table at Dan and, naively, perhaps, thought that with my background in theater, radio and writing, along with my work ethic, it would only be a matter of time before I broke in. I wanted to direct, act, produce, write. I wanted it all. And I knew Dan did, too. So I said, "Why not?" We went to bed that night giddy with expectation.

About ten days before we left for L.A., we had our friends Tina and Mark over for dinner. I had made some vaguely Indian thing with curry, lamb and quinoa that was meant to be wrapped in spelt tortillas because my acupuncturist, David, wanted me to eat more clarified butter and lamb, less wheat and chicken. Dan had already packed a huge pile of books into apple boxes, but everything else was status quo.

I remember looking around our rented 1,700-square-foot open loft space, with an office for me and a studio space for Dan, and thinking the chances of us finding anything like this in L.A. were slim. I loved that apartment. It was the most like a home of anywhere I'd ever lived in my adult years; we had a washer and dryer in the basement, tons of space to spread out and have dinner parties and celebrations, a little yard with a potted flower and herb garden and lots of wall space for art. My favorite thing, though, was the view from the bedroom that looked out into a little tangle of sweet briar bushes whose berries attracted a throng of English sparrows all year long, and beyond those I could see a small sliver of the majestic Atlantic Ocean. There were irritations like the three twenty-something girls who lived upstairs and all had boyfriends, which meant there were six people walking around on our heads all day and night, not to mention their drunken weekend parties. Also, our landlord, who was starting to feel the pinch from exorbitant heating oil prices for her buildings and the crunch of the economy, was making noises about raising the rent. And we could no longer afford the $1,200 we were already committed to.

During dinner we told Tina and Mark that we were planning to leave Portland and head northeast to my mother's on the coast for a few days to say goodbye. From there we'd take off across the country.

Mark looked at Dan and said, "What are you, nuts? If you go home to her mother's, Cait'll cry all the way to Indiana. Leave under cover of darkness, man. Blindfold her and leave." Mark was speaking from experience because he had brought Tina from New Mexico to Maine and away from her family. Apparently Tina *did* cry all the way to Indiana. She says she still can't get the image out of her head of her mother standing at the end of their long driveway, waving as they left.

There was something about this image of Tina's mom that went right through me. I sat there with my lamb, ghee and vegetable curry wrap and realized it's always been difficult for me to leave my mother. When I was a very small child and my parents' marriage already had the hairline fractures that would eventually split them apart, I was afraid of losing her. I thought she might just walk away and abandon our family. I don't know why I focused on her, specifically, but I guess that there was a larger sense of unrest I was keying into. The fact that I felt this still hurts my mother, because she says she was one hundred percent there for me in a difficult situation and that leaving Aran and me was out of the question.

Since the dissolution of my parents' marriage when I was eighteen, I became a person who worried about my mother being alone. It's not that this was warranted. My mother could have chosen a male companion if she had wanted to. But she didn't. So, I worried. My concerns didn't make me want to live with her, or even live that close by, and my guess is that she, too, would have had little interest in my hovering or pretending at caretaking. Since the divorce, having me home, even for vacations, brought her closer to my father because, obviously, I'd spend time going back and forth between their houses. And this created friction between us.

When I moved to Portland after over ten years of living in Paris; Providence; Cambridge, Massachusetts; and then New York City, I felt I had somehow, if inadvertently, chosen to be closer to my mother. My brother, Aran, was living in Miami by then and eventually moved to Mexico City with his wife, Margot. Our family felt disparate. I wanted to remedy that. My mother was three hours away—which, at that time, I felt, was the appropriate buffer any reasonable person should have from her parents. With this three-hour space between us, we had forged an easier closeness. It wasn't perfect. We still seemed to lack a baseline of settled trust that could afford the tensions of an argument. Instead we weathered periodic ruptures and silences and then we'd go back to our relationship as if nothing had happened. But the closeness we did have, I didn't want to lose. I realize, as I tell it here, that I didn't feel worried about leaving my father the same way. But he and I have always had a facile rapport. We can be totally present with each other on the phone, in e-mails or in person. And we rarely fight. Once, we spent an entire week together in Paris just eating and looking at art and talking about little else. It was the kind of blissful pause in life you imagine a vacation to be. But with my mother it's always been a more delicate balancing act. I think some of this is what happens in a divorce: You watch your parents disappear into their own personal hells and when they reappear, seeming slightly hungover from what they've been through, you're not sure they can see you. My mother and I had done a big chunk of repair work on our relationship when, one spring while I was still living in New York City, she took me to a dude ranch outside the Chiricahua Mountains in Arizona. It was there, driving across the desert, hiking into the shrubby, purple mountains, that some ease started to come back. It was there that I learned that I usually do best with her one-on-one—taking trips, spending weekends together, being a part of each other's lives in a more intense, important manner. My living closer to home had given us this more regularly; moving three thousand miles away was going to make this harder.

Regardless of my anxieties about leaving my mother, she gave us her blessing. She knew we were eager to get ahead in our careers and to chase some dreams, and she was excited about our adventure.

Right before we left, she came down for the Easter weekend and helped us pack our lives into boxes. Just three and a half years earlier she had helped me unpack my life into an apartment in Portland; now she was helping me leave. We went together to an Easter service at a small community church down the street and listened to the wonderful, soulful, gospel choir. She brought us an Easter basket of fruit and chocolate for our trip. We had plans to make a holiday dinner in the mess of our apartment, but this turned out to be impossible given that all our pans and china were en route with the movers to California. So, my mother bought us coffees and turkey-and-chutney sandwiches from a neighborhood sandwich shop and walked Hopper around the block for us (only to have the unfortunate experience of him lunging to greet another dog and lifting her off her feet so that she soared through the air like Mary Poppins and then fell back down onto the hard pavement. She came home holding her right forearm as if it were an injured bird). She stayed until the movers came and left. Then she left, too. When she drove off, her right hand still black and blue from her tumble on the pavement, it suddenly hit me that I might not see her for some time and that I was moving very far away. As I watched her shift, turn the corner and disappear, my throat got that odd strangled ache it gets when tears seem to be seeping throughout my whole body. The child in me wanted to run after her car and hug her once more, just in case. But I didn't.

For the few days after my mother left and before we finally hit the road, Dan and I slept on the floor on a blow-up mattress, cleaned our apartment, gave away our plants, tied up loose ends and came to terms with the reality that our lives had already moved. We just needed to join them.

On the night we left, although we hadn't eaten dinner and even though I wanted to hold on by my fingernails until morning when I thought Dan and I might be more levelheaded about taking this leap into shadowy unknowables, we stuck to our plan.

Dan was driving with a basket with all our vitamins in it between his feet. I was holding my jewelry box, filled with things I had inherited from both grandmothers, on my lap and had nowhere to put my feet. We drove like this, with Ellison wide-eyed and not making a peep and Hopper panting and freaking out in the backseat, until Massachusetts. There, about two hours from our now empty apartment, I realized, *This is really happening.*

There was no going back; just the shiny black macadam of unfolding change and new everything. We, like generations of Americans before us, were going west.

I was thirty-three years old and my life was beginning. Though not, it would turn out, in any of the ways I expected.

CHAPTER 4

A merica stretched out beyond our windshield, undiscovered by us—huge, exciting and full of possibility.
Next to me, driving, always driving and never letting
me drive, was my husband. In the backseat, perched atop piles
of our things were my cat of thirteen years and our two-year-
old dog, their eyes trained on us, the two people they trusted
to make choices that protected and cared for them.

As I remember it, the three-and-a-half-hour drive from Portland to Providence, Rhode Island, where we stopped for the
night, felt like the longest leg of our journey west.

As we drove I was thinking about how, over one hundred
and fifty years ago, couples just like us had started going west.
I remembered a story I'd read a long time ago of a pioneer leaving upstate New York with her husband. They sold all their
things; gave the dog to her mother; piled nice silver and linens,
family heirlooms and practical things into a covered wagon;

and left behind a cook, a maid and a parlor that looked out at a pear tree. She wrote about saying goodbye to her mother and how she guessed they might not see each other again until heaven and how that leave-taking was excruciating. Yet she soldiered on. Goodness, what hardship awaited her. She had no idea, with her silver, linens and nice dresses packed so neatly, what was coming or how many of those things she'd end up leaving on the side of the wagon track at the mouth of Donner Pass.

By the time we pulled into a motel and started unpacking our car, I felt small in a big world. We were hungry because we'd missed dinner and we were tired and frayed. We both took hot showers, put on clean underwear and I sat down on the bed with my computer and began a letter to a few family and friends. It was late, so I knew I couldn't call anyone, but I wanted to reach out and tell a handful of those closest to us that we were fine and had gotten over the wrenching hump of leaving. I wrote:

> Dear Family and Closest Friends,
> So, we packed up the last bits of our lives and got into the car and left today. It was not without some duress. . . . It's almost 1:30 AM. We're at a Holiday Inn. We never got dinner . . . and we're in a town called Warwick outside of Providence . . . Our friends Joelle and Brian and Molly and Frank and Chris and Tina and Mark all helped us so much to get going. Mom came and packed and got coffee and was Mary Poppins. If it weren't for you all we'd never

have gotten out of there. AND Dan was seriously
single mindedly focused. I was ready to put my head
under the covers and forget this was happening . . .
but Dan packed the covers. Bedtime now. I love you all.
I'm hoping tomorrow has blue skies. C.

After I e-mailed my missive, we made tea in our hot pot and,
blessedly, after that kind of stunned silence that can happen
between two people when an enormous life-changing event has
occurred, we fell asleep. I didn't know yet that I would continue
e-mailing letters home throughout our journey west and beyond
and that they would turn into a blog and that the blog would
not be a one-way communication from me to family and friends
but the opening up of a two-way stream of thoughts and support, eventually from people I didn't even know. I didn't yet
know that this journey we were making would one day become
a passage for my readers, too. But I did know that the connection was forged. Just writing a few words to those I loved back
home made me feel safer, somehow, as we left everything we
knew.

Hopper stayed awake all night, his ears perked to every
sound that came near our room, keeping watch, through the
window, on our car. Once, I awoke, the moonlight filling our
hotel room, to see Hopper standing on the radiator, his bulk
as enormous and wild as a wolf, growling at a leaf fluttering
outside.

When I got up at seven thirty, my eyes puffy and sealed
shut with the salt crust of seeping tears, I opened my computer
and found my inbox had new mail:

I hope you write one of these every day. I love
all four of you. Call me today -Love, Mom
p.s. Yes, blue skies today

"The course of true love never did run smooth."
—Shakespeare
"Moving across the country is a bitch."
—Me. . . . Love, Craig

Glad to hear from you and I'm relieved because
I've been thinking about you all night and wondering
how far you drove before calling it quits. I'm proud
of you two . . . Dan stuck to the plan and if it wasn't
for him you'd still be in that giant apartment with the
asshole land lord and that dick of a dog, Skip.
    Relax, remember, try to feel the future, and smile.
SMILE.
SMILE.
Love, Brian and Molly

Hi! Oh . . . I am so sorry about the problems! U
guys are troopers! :) Glad you got on the road and you
are headed to your great new future. Just remember
it is not the destination but the journey! :) This will
make your relationship stronger. I am thinking about
you both and sending you positive energy! Keep me
posted! Be safe . . . Tina

You're off. Oh that bold, bright sunshine seeping
into your bones and perking up those gray cells.

I wonder if The Johns—Ford and Steinbeck—
realize, up in them there pearlies, how many moving
stories they have inspired.—Aunt Maggie

———————

Great writing, Hon.
Very funny.
Hope you keep a journal of the trip.
Love, Dad

After reading these out loud to Dan and sniffling a bit, I
looked around our gray and beige hotel room and knew I needed
to get it together. I asked Dan to bring every single bag up from
the car and I proceeded to unpack everything onto the bed and
scrutinize each item. I made a huge pile of things—a Kenneth
Cole raincoat (how often does it really rain in L.A.?), a second
pair of white Gap corduroys (I'd loved these so much I'd bought
two pairs on clearance), jeans I could part with, shirts, sweaters,
shoes, socks—anything that I questioned, I was now willing to
get rid of. Dan and I were finally on the same page. Soon I had
an enormous black garbage bag of things that could go. It was
them or us and I chose the living, breathing beings and their
comfort in the car over the stuff. I also made a pile of things that
could be thrown out—junk that seemed to have been packed for
no real reason; underwear I wouldn't miss (do you, too, keep
around old underwear that seems like an insult to put on every
day?); an old New Yorker with an article I thought I might read
on the trip; a pair of Dan's socks I figured I might darn as we
drove (see how embedded the Pioneers were in my sense of going
west? I was even going to sew); an almost empty deodorant that

I wanted to *totally* finish before I opened the new one; two bottles of vitamin C that could easily be married; a couple of out-of-date guidebooks that I thought would be interesting to read on the way (but given that I had packed the entire Little House on the Prairie series and get easily carsick, how much reading time was I really going to have?), that kind of thing. This isn't quite like the heirlooms the pioneers needed to unload in order to get their wagons over Donner Pass, but we, too, needed to shed some of ourselves in order to forge ahead.

When we left the Holiday Inn parking lot that morning, the huge bag of things to take to the Salvation Army on my lap, I felt immensely lighter. After making our donation, we grabbed a couple of falafel sandwiches from a stand on Thayer Street that makes the best falafel wraps I've ever had in my life (hummus, hot peppers, pickles, baba ghanoush, vegetables and tahini sauce all in a huge, fluffy, homemade pita) and sat outside on the grass of one of Brown's capacious lawns, the sun dappling our backs and Hopper panting contentedly. In one last effort to begin again with order, I pulled a few bits of trash out of the car, ran a napkin over the dashboard, found every stray coin and put them all in the middle console for tolls and arranged an old piece of sheepskin on my seat to make our modern wagon more cozy. I made sure the animals were as comfortable as they could get and then we hit the road. Our iconic American trip was beginning, once again, with lots of leg room and a new attitude.

That first real day of travel, we arrived in D.C. late at night. We decided to drive down the dark, already leafy streets and take a tour past the Lincoln Memorial, the White House and the Washington Monument (not necessarily in that order, because we had a few moments of confusion when we were not sure if this, in front of us, really *was* the White House or some other big white house with lots of guards and then we had a big fight about it and felt like total hayseeds). Even in the dark, the majesty of our white buildings and gray stone structures, shining with a post-rain sheen, belied the pain of a country embroiled in two endless wars, beginning a devastating recession, with many of its values and laws so desperately challenged that the people were morally lost and defeated. The alabaster monuments stood, powerfully silent.

Dan said, "I hope I never get this close to George Bush again," and we both halfheartedly chuckled, because the purpose of our journey west and the place we found ourselves in as a nation really were sobering facts. After a few phone calls we discovered a Doubletree Hotel that would take all of us, four- and two-footed alike. We lugged our things inside, scarfed down the sugary, warm chocolate chip cookies that come with a Doubletree room, and I wrote a few lines to family and friends:

> As darkness came this evening, slow and thick like a
> fog over the wastelands of New Jersey, I began to
> realize, in the pit of my stomach, the enormity of
> what we're doing. This is no small gesture, no small
> trip, no road vacation. . . . Hopper, Ellison, Dan and
> I are all alike: vessels of hope and fear whirling into
> the darkness with only each other to cleave to.
>
> We miss you all tonight and love you.
> Cait & Dan

That was the thing: We really did feel like we were alone, just the four of us, in our small car on big highways and in places where the only beings we knew were each other. There was a freedom, though, that came with the car as our base, which by its nature is always rolling somewhere—a freedom I had never experienced before. There was also, naturally, a searching quality. America was becoming ours because each place we went for the first time we were seeing with fresh eyes and open hearts. Each town we stopped in we wondered, "Could we make a home here?" And each night in each motel, no matter how dingy, we put everything inside with care, planning how we'd organize our gear, pet bowls, litter box and beds so that the animals had everything they needed and we could all feel somewhat at home, if only for a night.

That next morning in D.C., Dan went out and got us coffee, sat down with a huge atlas of America in front of him and started planning the next leg of our trip. Then, after a Thai lunch around the corner from our hotel, we left the familiar eastern seaboard behind and began heading southwest through the Blue Ridge Mountains and into the heartland of America.

Although we had hoped to get as far as Asheville, North Carolina, that night, after a meandering drive through horse country and farms, trailer parks and suburban sprawl, we hit Charlottesville and it started raining. So, Dan decided our travel would be faster if we could get across the Blue Ridge Mountains and head south that way. When I offered to drive, for the first time yet on our trip, Dan relented.

By then it was starting to get dark and it was raining hard. Before we knew it, our hatchback was blowing around next to eighteen-wheelers on a highway lined with flares that signaled terrifying drops into oblivion on one side and large, imperious mountains on the other. Our car, unhappy at such altitudes, began heaving and bellowing. The animals, who had been too stressed to go to the bathroom since Maine, even with numerous walks around leafy patches of ground and many introductions to the litter box, were now miserable. In the dark, our resolve started to flag. (Isn't that always the way? You can get up in the a.m. and the world can seem full of blue skies and unending vistas, and then it gets dark and suddenly you feel like you're in the middle of a Hieronymous Bosch painting.) When we finally cascaded out of the foggy mountains onto I-81—a large, straight highway that shoots right down the side of Appalachia—we were so tense, it was as if we had survived a near-death experience. Wanting nothing more than sleep, I asked Dan to call some of the motels in our book *Vacationing with Your Pet*. I have this irritating tendency to tell Dan what to say on the phone sometimes, which only makes him grumpy and me sound like the world's most annoying person piping up in the background. So, when he followed my neurotic neat-freak lead and asked one woman on the other end if her rooms were clean, there was a stunned silence. And then, in her Virginia drawl, she answered, "Well, sir, it's not the Hilton if that's what you mean." Dan took a room. Quickly and apologetically.

Indeed it was not the Hilton. It was the kind of motel you might see in a horror movie, with dimly lit halls, an empty swimming pool in the center of a breezeway and human urine reeking in corners of the parking lot. Our room was tidy enough but smelled so strongly of chemical cleaning products that even with *Psycho* images running through our minds, we had to sleep with the windows open. That night I wrote to friends and family:

> Tomorrow we're getting up early, out of this motel and we'll beat it to Asheville where not only Mom's father, my grandfather, Trav, went to the Asheville School for Boys, but also my surrogate granddad, Ken. We'll be calling Ken tomorrow AM when we drive down the street where he grew up and hearing where he had his first kiss. Hopper's guarding the door. Ellison's holding hands with Dan. Goodnight, we love you. C & D, H & E.

The next morning I sat in bed with my "complimentary breakfast" of weak coffee and a spongy bagel and read the next installment of responses to my letter home. After showers and packing up, we started cruising through the shaggy Appalachian Mountains, stopping every so often for Dan to photograph. At the base of the foothills, the same big-box stores that have spread like invasive weeds across all of America and beyond littered what was once the unbridled wild. In one town a McDonald's had replaced the local general store—which was across the street and boarded up—and everyone came in and greeted one another with good afternoons, asked about each other's health and families and then ordered coffee and McNuggets. There were times, driving through the mess

we've collectively made of some of the most beautiful country
you've ever seen, that America seemed like a hopeless place. By
that I mean that when you see the devastation done to the land
by corporate shopping strips and highways, you wonder, What
happened to our small towns? If we have no small towns and no
community, does America have any future at all? Where are our
purple mountains and fruited plains? Later that night I would
write in my letter home that Dan had turned to me somewhere
in that corner where Tennessee meets North Carolina and Virginia and said, "I feel kind of homesick for Maine."

We did feel homesick. Maine, more like a family member
than a state, sears through your heart no matter how annoying
you find the snow and icy temperatures that seem to last six
months of the year only to give way to two months of mud season. There's something about being from Maine that you can
never let go of—the pointed firs and feathery pine trees, the wide
open sky and stars and moon on a cold night, the ocean, which
smells of this wonderful mix of saline and savory, and the
colors—deep golds and reds and browns in the fall lit against a
perfect blue sky; the lush, wet greens of summer and clean, white
snow of winter piled against dark, stoic evergreens. And there are
the people: a mix of briny Mainers who will keep their emotional
distance but if they see you off the side of the road in a snowbank
will jump out of their trucks and tow you with chains (which
they, of course, have on hand) without a second's thought. There
are also all the "people from away" who are transplants, many
with the uncanny tendency to always be some kind of artist, who
have embraced the land and the place with a love that inspires
some wonderful art and music, plays and novels.

As we got farther and farther away from home, America

seemed so big and bruised and foreign that our sense of who we were felt complicated by each mile we traversed. And it was this complication, possibly, that made the journey worth it. As we went, we were becoming citizens of America, really, not just of one place, one state, one town. We were witnessing our selves and our hopes, dreams and goals against the backdrop of places and people we didn't know or even, maybe, relate to. This rootlessness kept us wonderfully open to seeing and experiencing everything around us with the freshness of babies.

All the way to Asheville, a town full of old, funky buildings, restaurants, coffee watering holes and mom-and-pop shops selling hemp clothes and folk art, we were listening to Dolly Parton and singing our lungs out to "Coat of Many Colors," "Applejack" and "Jolene." We found an outdoor café where we could sit with Hopper and ate a plate of fried onion rings and big, juicy burgers. Sated, we piled back into the car and went out to find my surrogate granddad's childhood house. Ken and Cherie had befriended my parents soon after we moved from Gouldsboro to our new home. After some years, they adopted me as their de facto grandchild when my father's parents died, just after I graduated from college (my mother's parents had died when I was three). I had named Cherie and Ken Meme and Poppop. We found Poppop's old Southern home on a red horse chestnut–lined street, the lawns neatly mown, the bushes pruned. He and Meme both got on the line as we described every detail, then we took pictures, which we e-mailed later that night. This moment of sharing Poppop's past in our present, as we imagined him living in this stately house as a boy, warmed and tethered us as we got back in the car and headed farther south.

Late at night we pulled into Montgomery, Alabama, the

heart of the Civil Rights Movement and the Deep South. In the dark we found a motel that would take us and our pets and unloaded our gear into a room that was a dismal combination of greasy brown and algae green. Ellison found a dead cockroach on the floor and outside, closer to the edge of the parking lot, Hopper found a dead rabbit. Hopper also met a small, white dog named Tommy. When Dan asked if Hopper could say hello, his owner answered, "Tommy duddent play wid strangers."

That night I wrote again to the folks back home. By now I'd picked up a few more readers, my missives being circulated to friends of friends and some people I didn't know had requested to be put on my list. I wasn't sure why anyone cared, but the enthusiasm to share this trip with us inspired me and I wanted to keep writing. I kept my postings as letters because I felt safer writing to the few people whose faces I imagined: my parents and family, our friends.

> Tomorrow we hope to make it to Houston. I can't
> believe I'm saying this, but I kind of want to get to
> Texas . . . Good night and . . . good luck to me to get a
> wink of sleep whilst knowing there might be dead bugs
> and rabbits and who knows what else just beyond these
> sheets. Love, C, D, H & especially Ellison, the lowest
> maintenance and sweetest traveling companion.

After very little sleep and even less circulating air, we got up the next morning and drove out to find a good cup of coffee. This was harder than you might think. From the outside, to a passerby, Montgomery is a curious city. Upon entering the downtown area we passed a huge billboard with a picture of a handgun that said STOP THE VIOLENCE IN MONTGOMERY. Driving around, we couldn't find anything that was open for breakfast. Boarded up shops; a crumbling gas station that looked like it had not been in operation since 1960; pawn, bail bond and junk shops lined the streets. A gleaming, immaculately restored White House of the Confederacy rose in the center of downtown. I wondered if this was a town that was lived somewhere else, like in the suburbs? Or was it that since the Civil Rights Movement, not a penny had been spent on keeping the city alive and vibrant? Or were we just in the wrong part of town and missing something? As we meandered up the streets looking for at least a coffee cart, we were getting more and more desperate. Suddenly, a government car pulled up next to us and the driver rolled down his window and leaned out toward our car with a big smile. When we opened our window, he asked, "Are you folks lost?"

"Well, we're hungry," Dan said. "And a little frantic for a cup of coffee."

"Nah, you won't find anything like that down here. And you folks might consider not hanging around too much in any one spot in these parts. Not safe. The only thing I can recommend is the Wendy's back by the highway."

Dan, incredulous, said, "There's no coffee or breakfast anywhere in downtown Montgomery?" We had envisioned steaming plates of grits with fried eggs and bacon.

"No, sir."

Dan pushed further, his caffeine headache by now making him truculent (one thing anyone can tell you about Dan is that he drinks buckets of coffee and likes nothing better than a rainy day with Greg Brown on the stereo, a huge pot of coffee on his desk and some photos to make). "How is that possible? There has to be a coffee shop somewhere here?"

"Just the way it is, sir." And the man drove off, his government tags winking at us as he went. Whether what he'd told us was true or this guy had some other agenda, we will never know. Heeding his words about danger, however, because who can handle fear when they are half asleep and hungry, we drove to the fast food mecca he had described and found ourselves in line at Chick-fil-A. Every sandwich, in case you've never eaten at one of these fine establishments, has some version of fried chicken on it—even the breakfast sandwiches. After a confusing back and forth that mostly involved monosyllabics, we ascertained that we'd missed the breakfast window by ten minutes and needed to order lunch. Fine. I implored Dan to ask what comes on the Chick-fil-A sandwich.

"Excuse me, ma'am, could you tell me what comes on the Chick-fil-A? What condiments?"

Silence.

"Excuse me, ma'am, are there any condiments on the Chick-fil-A, or . . . is there lettuce?"

"Pickle, sir."

"Just one pickle?"

Silence.

"Ma'am, is there anything else on it besides a pickle?"

"Pickle."

"OK, can we get some lettuce and mayo on it?"

Silence.

"And two Cokes?"

Silence.

"Excuse me, but did you get our order?"

"Yes."

More silence.

"Would you like me to drive up?"

Silence.

"Excuse me, but would you like me to drive up?"

"Sir, that will be twelve eighty-five."

My sandwich came with exactly one pickle and no lettuce or mayo. Dan, who'd ordered the Chick-fil-A Deluxe, got the tomato and lettuce. However, both sandwiches, wrapped in foiled paper, were soggy. Despite our hunger, we threw them out around the corner and pushed on farther south until Mobile, where we found a Starbucks for coffee and bagels and made peanut-butter-and-potato-chip bagel sandwiches from our picnic basket. Fortified, we pushed on through the wilds of Mississippi, the road long and straight in the hot spring sun, a jungle of dark, swampy, overgrowing kudzu clinging to the sides of the tarmac.

We took I-10 through New Orleans and up to Baton Rouge, where we stopped in a parking lot to let Ellison out of her carrier in the car so that she could stretch her legs and eat. We walked Hopper by the Mississippi River. And, then, even though it was late, we decided to cross the Mississippi. It was then, after making that epic crossing of a river that looms large and significant not only in American history books but also in our memories of Huck Finn, that the trip seemed to really take on a feeling of freedom. It's impossible, as you start driving across the South, hit Texas and then push on farther west, to ignore every road trip story from *On the Road*, *The Grapes of Wrath* and *My Ántonia* to *Thelma & Louise* and

Rain Man. These stories hover somewhere between you and the windows of your car so that, as if wearing 3D glasses, you see an overlay of your journey and the journeys of your favorite fictional characters in your imagination as you go. You add American music—some bluegrass or country, jazz or blues— as your soundtrack and you've got your own film in which you're the star. Even though it was dark, as we drove with Bruce Springsteen's Seeger Sessions on the iPod, we could see that the bayou in Louisiana was full of the gray limbs of cypress trees, tangly and more like huge serpents rearing out of the water than just mere trees. We saw truck stops and gas stations, refineries and then the lights of our first big western city in the distance.

At three a.m. we found a Holiday Inn in downtown Houston. Our animals were grateful to get off the road. We all climbed into bed together, Ellison taking her rightful spot between my legs and Hopper nestling between me and Dan. That night I wrote home:

It's 3 AM. I'm exhausted. Dan's asleep.

The next morning I woke up to this note from Dan's friend Frank:

Dear Pickles & Frychicken-
I have received all of your road chronicles.
Wicked entertaining.

Hopefully more stories of your awkward, bizarre
encounters will result in my continued amusement.
Drive safely and bring your own damn
condiments.—F

And there were more requests for my e-mails home:
"Honey, Norman and Paula want to be added to the list. Love,
Mom." "Caitlin, I heard about your letters home from Frank,
can you put me on your list?!" "Hi Cait, your Dad forwarded me
your last letter. Can I get these?" "Hi Caitlin, you don't know
me, but three years ago I came out to New Mexico from the
East Coast. I love your story. Would you add me?" Since the
circle seemed to be widening, I decided to start a blog, where I
could begin posting my entries. So began what I like to call my
"epistolary blog."

After drinking tall coffees, which Dan had fetched from a
nearby coffee shop, we slowly packed up and hit the road
again. The funny thing about driving long distances like this
is that despite the fact that you are doing absolutely no physical activity (unless you consider eating fast food an exercise),
your body actually begins to ache and get tired as if you've been
riding a horse across the prairie all day.

In Texas, as the land opened up to wide vistas; delicate
spring grasses swaying in the wind; and meadows covered with
bluebonnets, pink poppies and clover, horses, cows and sheep,
the sheer expanse of America was starting to sink in. We were
only halfway across the country and we still had Texas, which

is larger than the entire country of France, to cross. I began to think of Texas as our gateway to the west—you must cross it in order to get to the southwest and to California. It is huge and hot, arid across the western part of the state, and, in some ways, Texas feels lawless despite the fact that it executes more inmates than any other state in the union. There's a swagger in Texas, though, which is seductive. Maybe it's because almost all the trucks have guns in the back of the cabs, which reminds me of Maine (Maine, also a hunting state, has a large per capita gun-to-person ratio). There are those four short lines in Lyle Lovett's song "North Dakota" that encapsulate, for me, the spirit of Texas: "And the cowboys down in Texas/They polish up their guns/And they look across the border/To learn the ways of love."

We saw people in Texas pull up to a general store in their trucks, leave them running, get out and let the doors stand open while they went inside to get some beef jerky and cigarettes. I thought, Well, there's a sexy confidence! That no-holds-barred, screw-borders-and-rules bravado was titillating. Maybe this innate sexy Texan-ness is why America bought George W. Bush? I, for one, didn't expect to love Texas. I anticipated being repelled by anything that reminded me of Bush. In the Northeast, during Bush's tenure, "Texas" had become a dirty word, a joke. But it was here on these wide open plains that my inner cowgirl woke up and my weakness for cowboys and horses, ranches and cattle, dry air and hot sun, Americana in all its big, blustery home-on-the-range-show-no-shame forthrightness all came roaring out of me like something that had been trapped for a long, long time. I was giddy with joy the entire three days it took us to cross Texas. I loved it that much.

After miles and miles of beautiful ranches that spread out wide and undaunted by the huge sky and open air, we dove into Austin, a town full of art and good coffee, rockabilly hipsters and cowboy artists. At Jo's, an outdoor coffee shop, we met up with Dan's friend Nicky's parents, who bought us tall iced coffees and gave Dan a carefully bubble-wrapped jar of Nicky's grandmother's famous hot sauce. That night we gorged on Southwest Mexican food until, late at night, we pulled out and continued west. When I remember all this now I am astounded and personally chagrined at the patience of our animals during all this stopping and driving and long stretches of time in the car. Ellison, in particular, was relegated to hours upon hours alone in the car, waiting for us as we ate meals and discovered new places and then endured more hours of driving on top of that. "At least they're with us," Dan would say when I worried about their little hearts so wide open with wonder and confusion at what in the world we were doing, "They're home with us. They know that."

In *Little House on the Prairie*, when Pa takes his family west, Jack, their dog, walks beneath the wagon wheels the whole time and never once complains. Hopper would never in a million years stand for that. He'd want to be in the wagon with the girls, licking a pan of rabbit stew from dinner and laying his head on a pillow. Their cat, Black Susan, undoubtedly gets left behind; she disappears from the narrative. That's the thing about books—a pet can be a character for the first two hundred pages and then a divorce happens or someone dies and you never hear about that animal again. I've always hated that, when the animal just vanishes from the story. Our animals, though, were right there with us in the backseat. Hopper was perched, his ears cocked like Henry Fonda wearing a slouch cap the whole way, and Ellison was nestled in her little cage, her bed a nest made of little bits of an old fur jacket I got at a thrift shop, and surrounded by toys and catnip. Sometimes, in the sun, Ellison would lie on her back and warm her belly, purring loudly. Despite how hard this must have been on her, Ellison loved us all being together like this, crammed into one spot, no one going off anywhere. She always liked having everyone where she could see them.

That night we stayed in a motel in a tiny trucking town called Sonora. The next morning, we crossed wide, dry scrubland for miles upon miles. We stopped in a frontier town called Van Horn for lunch at a Tex-Mex dive called Chuy's that was a self-described "hall of fame" for the former football star John Madden, a football commentator for decades who refused to fly and often found himself eating rice and beans at Chuy's while catching a game on their big TVs. While we were eating some delicious beans and tortillas, our moving company called to tell us that our things were arriving in L.A. the very next day. Our food barely digested, we went into panic mode because we were not there yet and had signed a contract that gave us fifteen days to meet our belongings ("You tell us the date, we'll have it there when you need it!"). It hadn't even been ten days. They told us that we were going to have to pay more now for them to hold our boxes while we made it across the country. Somehow, despite what was agreed on paper, there was a loophole. And they told us there was now a delivery charge because the street where our new apartment was located was too narrow to unload, despite being four lanes wide. We understood then that every angle of this moving outfit was crooked.

Suddenly anxious to get to our belongings, we pressed on and made it to El Paso by dinnertime. There we bought some cowboy boots at a "Cowboy Boot Outlet," fed the animals in the car and decided to keep driving across New Mexico to Tucson. In the dark, we crossed the desert, with only the camaraderie of trucks on the highway and trains whistling past. The temperature dove to fifty-four degrees and Ellison started making noises and turning around in her cage. At first I wasn't sure if she needed to poop or pee, or if it was the fresh, cold desert air. But then I realized, "She's lonely! She's been back there in her cage day after day for almost a week. She wants physical contact." I opened the small door and pulled her onto my lap and she spent the next few hours of the night cuddling and purring, peering out the window at the big sky as we drove straight into Orion's belt.

In Tucson we were lucky enough to get a lovely room in an inn that allowed pets and was furnished with a clean white comforter and a plumped bed. Nestled in, my family around me, I wrote that being so close to our destination made our homesickness feel that much more present:

> To have the kind of friends who help us pack, give
> us cash to go, call us, send us names of friends to
> connect with in LA . . . who help us leave . . . well,
> seriously, there is no kindness in my life I've
> experienced quite like this. You know who you are,
> you know what I mean. I love you and I'm so
> incredibly grateful.

We slept soundly that night and awoke to sunny, blue skies on our last morning on the road. My mother had written in, as she did every morning, to my most recent post:

> Sweetie, you are right, the movers are crooked. And they have you over a barrel. After you get your stuff—maybe report them? Take them to small claims court? Think of taking a day to recover in Tucson you love that city (despite the damned movers). BUT WEAR SUNBLOCK . . . Also please let Dan drive— you are not a very careful driver and you scare me when you drive. Cuddle with Ellison, bless her heart.
>
> Love, Mom

After lunch at a street fair near the university we began the last leg of our trip. We passed long vistas of cacti as far as we could see, went through Yuma, crossed the muscled border where California touches Mexico and dove into the darkness of evening. As we made our way across the Santa Rosa Mountains, the wind tossed our car around. Finally we dipped down, the lights of San Diego below us, the enormous Pacific beyond. California was resplendent. It sparkled in the dark like a jewel box filled with gold.

CHAPTER 5

When you've crossed the whole country and truly come to the end of land, the end of the United States of America, and have seen the Pacific Ocean, there's nothing quite like it. You feel small and enormous at once, impotent and invincible by turns. It was a Saturday night, April 5, and we'd been on the road for exactly a week. We hit L.A.'s Saturday night traffic, a sea of headlights and brake lights as far as the eye could reach, and to the right and left more lanes and highways all strung together and splitting off into the darkness, all aswarm with cars, each one filled with a life, some dreams, disappointments and a story. Dan looked at me, his face almost childlike in its grave innocence, and said, "Man, we're not in Maine anymore." I felt my stomach lurch a little, the way it does when someone mentions an old boyfriend you've finally stopped crying about.

Dan can remember how to get to places he's only been

once or twice, and, soon enough, he had us driving down Wilshire Boulevard and into Santa Monica until we saw the famous walkway filled with eucalyptus trees and beyond that the ocean crashing into the beaches. As he turned left from Wilshire onto Pacific, he tuned the iPod to Solomon Burke's version of "Millionaire," a song we'd embraced as our own personal anthem of love and endurance as we crossed America. As it began to play, Dan rolled down our windows, put the volume on high and we began to sing as loud as we could, giddy as teenagers, energized by this brazen journey we'd just succeeded at making:

> They say love is more precious than gold
> It can't be bought, and it can't be sold
> I got love . . . love to spare
> That makes me, a millionaire

It was after midnight and people were straggling home. In the anonymity a big city affords, no one even noticed our small car with Maine plates cruising down Pacific Avenue with a couple of crazed thirty-year-olds singing their lungs out. When the song was done, we played it again. And again. Until we got to Chairman Mao's, a Chinese place in Venice we'd been to before and is open until three a.m. (Isn't it funny how when you move to a new place you go immediately to what you know, thereby trying to establish your community from the get-go?) Dan jumped out and ran in to order us a mess of Chinese food for takeout while I waited with the animals, full of trepidations but excited to unpack in our new apartment. We'd found the place, at the last minute, a few days before we left, on the

Internet through a service called Westside Rentals. A friend of ours had checked it out, telling us it was small, which we expected given L.A. prices and what we could afford, but that it was clean and beautifully made. When Dan got back in the car, we turned on our theme song once more and drove the final five minutes to pull up in front of our new home.

W hat I saw first were their feet: Six huge, dirty, men's feet facing me in our headlights. Then I saw bodies. Hopper started growling from the backseat and Dan said, "There's someone sleeping in front of our apartment." "Someone" was a euphemism for "many someones," because it was, in fact, five people, three with their feet propped on our stoop. Surrounding them was a little encampment made of cardboard boxes, sleeping bags and shopping carts. Ah, the underbelly of the American Dream: We have no effective and humane solution to the homeless problem.

"Do we have the right apartment?" I asked Dan, my voice starting to rise.

"I think so. Just stay here. Let me get out."

"I don't want you getting out."

"Why, Caitlin? Don't be ridiculous. I'll handle this."

Deputy Dan got out of the car and pulled his deepest, most authoritative voice out of his chest: "Excuse me, sirs, this is our apartment. You need to go find somewhere else to sleep." He stood with his arms crossed, his face tight. In moments like these I love my husband. I know, because he's gentle and soft, sensitive and even fragile, sometimes, what it takes to put the armor back on that he wore for all those years as a kid from the trailer park. I know this toughness feels odd to his new skin and yet, when it comes to his family, he'd kill someone if he had to. This knife's edge of his where he can turn harsh and hard in a way that astounds even him, sometimes scares me, sometimes amazes me. But when it comes out, I know he means business and I've never seen anyone, even an insane homeless person, challenge him. These guys threw around a few rounds of "Fuck you, asshole!" and one guy threw his box on the ground, kicked at it and then picked it up again, tucking it under his arm. But they moved from the stoop. They stood for a second at the end of our parking lot, talking and glaring at Dan, who stared back. And then they walked across the street, where they stood watching us. Dan went into the apartment and looked around long enough to find that there was no electricity or water turned on, and came back out.

When he got into the car, he was putting on the best-case scenario for me, which, bless his heart, I sometimes wonder if he does for me, really, or for himself because his all-important plans have hit a major challenge and he'd like to pretend for a few more minutes that everything is totally copacetic. But I was already internally doing what Dan likes to call "hitting the puke button."

"Dan, this is a fucking disaster. Is that our front door, right there? There's no hall or anything? And it's made out of glass? So all we have is a thin sheet of glass between us and those homeless guys? What the fuck was Bill thinking? You're traveling for work next week; I can't stay here by myself. All those windows, right there, that's the living room, right level with the parking lot where these guys sleep every night? Man, were they pissed. I mean, this is *their* place. They're still watching us, see?" My head was spinning, my voice was cracking.

"The apartment is awesome, Cait. Really. It's small, but totally great. Come inside. The glass door . . . I don't know what to do about that. I need to think. Let's go in and eat our food. It's not that bad."

By now we were almost out of money. We'd sunk first month, last month and two months of rent for a security deposit into this apartment, most of which was money we'd been saving for months and gotten from our tax return. With the extra costs of the movers and our budget to get ourselves started in L.A., much of what we had left was space on credit cards. And we still needed to find work.

I could barely eat the greasy egg rolls on the paper plate Dan handed me. Ellison was wide-eyed and running around, sniffing every corner and Hopper stood growling at the glass door, daring anyone to just try. In the darkness, sitting on the floor with our Chinese food on our laps, we were able to see not only how tiny the place was, but also that the frosted-glass front door didn't quite touch the doorjamb. Although the apartment had beautiful wood floors and a stone shower and freshly painted white walls, our ground-level living room windows didn't quite close flush, leaving enough space for anyone to pry them open from the outside. Indeed, the sash of one of the kitchen windows had already been stretched by someone trying to get in. Also, in order to properly close our front door, we needed to lock it with the key from within or else it just swung open into the parking lot.

Our friend Bill, whom I'd met on a previous trip to L.A. and who'd offered to vet the place, is a single guy who can be a wonderful friend but, it turns out, an impractical thinker. He admitted, later, that he'd never paused to think about my being alone there and whether or not it was safe. He'd never considered the animals. He'd, also, never noticed a bathroom window that was stuck and broken open so that anyone could hoist himself inside our apartment at any hour of any day. Although he said he'd known about the homeless population on this corner, he hadn't, he said, put two and two together. Clearly, having someone else look at an apartment is one of the world's worst ideas. It would have been cheaper, in the end, to have flown out and chosen our own place, or, even, just found one once we landed. But we had wanted to get going. We had wanted a home. Anyway, hindsight as they say . . .

Finally, Dan asked me, "What do you want to do, Cait?"

"Well, we can't stay here."

"OK, we'll find a hotel."

Back in the safety of the car, I almost wanted to laugh. Or cry hysterically. It was two a.m. and I was beyond tired. When Dan got into the car, he sat down with a thud and put his head in his hands for a second and murmured, "Fuck, man. Just fuck. I need a beer." Unfortunately we were out of luck on that one, since sales had stopped at two.

We started driving around. At each hotel or motel one of us would get out, go in, ask if they took pets, come back to the car shaking our heads and then continue on. At three in the morning we found a La Quinta next to LAX Airport that would take the animals. After lugging all of our things in on a dolly, Dan turned on the news and I took a bath. Dan wanted to get a few hours of sleep so that he could think better in the morning. I knew sleep was unlikely. Instead I sent an e-mail to my friends and family to tell them we needed some help to think this one through: *I miss Texas! Any ideas? Love and miserably yours, Caitlin.* The animals, picking up on our anxiety, panted and moved around all night, never settling in. No one, not even Dan who can sleep while a bomb is detonated outside his window, got any shut-eye.

In the morning, a flurry of e-mails from family and friends came in offering solutions, thoughts and condolences. My surrogate grandparents, Meme and Poppop, offered to pay for our hotel expenses. Our friend Frank, Dan's best man, reminded us that what we're good at is solutions. That's what we needed to focus on, Frank said. "As Helen Keller once wrote," he reminded us,

"Life is either a daring adventure or nothing."
Do Not Give Up. —Frankie.

Inspired by his (and Helen Keller's) words, we showered and dressed. I put on some lipstick, a clean tank top and fresh jeans. One thing I've always believed is that when things start to go to hell in a handbasket, you might as well try to look good while it happens. It's amazing what a little lipstick, some mascara and a clean shirt will do to your outlook. By the time we piled into the car once again, I was feeling moderately competent to handle whatever needed to be examined. It was a brilliantly sunny morning and the wind had a crispness to it that felt like slices of cold, green Granny Smith apple on your arms. In Venice, we bought some breakfast sandwiches and coffee and walked Hopper to a nearby dog park so he could run around. At first, he was shy and gangly like a small child. But then he took off to play, eager to please. There was a moment there, with the sun and the dogs running, when things seemed moderately doable. We weren't going home, that was the truth. We were going to do this, even if it killed us. This is what happens when you cross oceans and continents to make new, brave starts in the world: You become vulnerable to everyone and everything and your true mettle gets tested.

Over the next few days we hunkered down at the La Quinta and made an inventory of the problems with the apartment, photographed the stuck window, the two-way latch door that was more appropriate for a shop than a residence, the bent guard rails and the space around the doorjamb, which left our apartment open to the elements and any varmint that might care to join us for dinner. We met a skinny older guy named Sam, who lived across the street. He was a predictable Venice type, always wearing black skinny jeans, his gray hair puffed into a pompadour and his dark-rimmed glasses glinting in the sun. Whenever he saw us he'd come down from his apartment, cross the street and tell us some new bit of salacious gossip about how bad the homeless problem was on this corner. He supplied us with vivid images of a single woman who lived two doors down and who, he insisted, had resorted to hiring bodyguards because the homeless people who slept on our steps kept having sex in her garden. He said that one homeless guy had threatened to burn the building down and that another was insane and violent and carried a knife. Dan laughed every time he saw Sam coming and said, "Oh boy, here comes the neighbor-hood blue-hair." But we were grateful to him for imparting the neighborhood lowdown.

When we finally met our landlord in person, he assured us that he hadn't known about the homeless problem and that he didn't think it was a very big deal. Then, as if on cue, a guy came up to the Dumpster outside our kitchen window. The landlord said, "Hey, move it along." The guy turned around, looked at him with a bored expression that said he'd been though this before, and said, "I'm just getting my clothes, ass-hole." And, indeed, he pulled a few things for that day's outfit out of our Dumpster. The landlord eventually agreed to let us out of the lease. The main argument Dan gave him was that I couldn't be left alone there; the landlord conceded that *maybe*, given the door and the window and the homeless situation, it *might not*, in the *worst possible scenario*, be the best place for a woman alone. He said he'd always felt this apartment was a great place for a single, surfing, twenty-year-old guy.

In the meantime, a friend found another friend named Penny, who had a cottage she was willing to rent to us on a weekly basis. Four days after arriving in Los Angeles, we moved all our things into a storage unit and began to set up shop in Penny's furnished cottage. From there we began trying to extricate some portion of our money from the landlord who, despite having agreed to let us out of our lease, hadn't also agreed to give us any money back. We filled Penny's fridge with farmer's market foods and tried to get some lay of the land, finding the nearest supermarket, drugstore and the French Market Café, a short walk from Penny's, where we could get great coffee and baguette sandwiches. And, also, we started to laugh. The whole thing, if you stopped to think about it, was hilarious and crazy. Sometimes, what other choice do you have but to laugh?

By Friday, we'd been at Penny's for three days and the world felt immensely sunnier, what with the laughing and great coffee from the French Market. We still hadn't gotten our money back, but I'd called the City of Los Angeles and found that many things in our apartment violated codes and, armed with that knowledge and some legalese from my lawyer uncle, Jay, I was prepared to get aggressive. This is where Dan and I often divide and conquer. He handles people face-to-face, I handle the written documents. That night as I drafted my first letter to our erstwhile landlord, Dan started packing to go back east for ten days to shoot for a woman's apparel company for a week followed by three days of shooting a documentary in Philly.

On Saturday, Dan and I went shopping to make sure the animals and I had enough food so we wouldn't have to navigate too much in our new city. He wanted to get everything organized so we'd be OK, even though I kept saying with false bravery, "We'll be fine!" As night drew in and his flight time inched closer, I missed him already. It's funny how your partner can be the one person who drives you the most nuts in the world, the one person you are the most awful to, the person who sees you most closely at your worst but is also the person without whom you'd feel like your life is entirely incomplete. Without Dan, as much as I hate to admit it, I'm a wreck. He tethers my life and my soul. And I'm crazy about him. That night, before I drove him to the airport in Long Beach to catch a JetBlue, we made love with an intensity reserved for soldiers leaving home for what might be forever.

During our lovemaking I felt this hot zing go through my body unlike any orgasm I'd ever had before. Later, as we were getting dressed I said, "I hope I was right about when I got my period," suddenly doubting my calculations and the riskiness of unprotected sex. "I might have forgotten about that five-day-sperm-living-inside-you rule my aunt Maggie told me about—but how could that even be true?" Then I counted the days on my fingers again. "No problem," I said with the assurance of a Planned Parenthood educator.

Dan just laughed and said, "Well, you know, that would be a positive negative."

I drove him down the 405 to the airport, drove back and pulled both Hopper and Ellison into the bed with me and wept. I missed him that much. I felt totally alone, way out west in a place I did not know and where I knew almost no one. As I fell asleep, a mockingbird in Penny's garden gabbed and laughed the night away.

CHAPTER 6

During the ten days Dan was gone, I was trying to find us an apartment. I figured that my approach should include Hopper, because he needed walks.

One morning Hopper and I found a place we liked. It was on a long palm tree and bougainvillea-lined avenue that reached to the post office at Venice Circle and then to the great Pacific beyond. At the front door stood a very old, wise-seeming palm tree whose wide-hipped base was covered with little orange morning glories, making it look like an older bride. Around the tree was a garden with white roses and deep orange canna lilies. The building itself was yellow stucco and had an open-air entryway with mailboxes. The apartment was on the ground floor. Inside, the floors were covered with red Mexican tiles, which reminded me of the tiles in my mother's kitchen and immediately made me feel at home. The apartment had no private space other than the bathroom, but I figured we could make it work because there was a tiny outdoor patio, which was almost like a whole other room. It wasn't quite big enough for a homesteader's garden, but it would be a lovely place for potted tomatoes, herbs and flowers. I imagined Ellison basking in the sunlight out there and thought, "We can really make this nice." When I filled out the application, I felt like "OK, great, things are starting!"

There was a hitch, though. The landlord, Jerry, said there was "a *kind of* daffy older lady" who'd be living above us, named Mabel. Jerry was one of those Venice, California, types who's in his fifties but whose hair has not yet started to visibly gray and is always wearing what Dan likes to call yoga culottes and an American Apparel version of the '80s muscle shirt. He drove a cherry red MINI Cooper and had been working on a doctoral dissertation about the fine art of Turkey for the last ten years. Jerry told me Mabel was more like the "concierge of the building" and that she'd been there for over thirty-five years. He did allow that she was "sort of crazy" but "well meaning," sometimes "might drink a little too much" and every so often would "yell." OK, I was desperate for us to have an apartment in Venice Beach and I wanted our lives to start coming together after the disaster that unraveled the moment we made it across the country, but I'm not *such* a big idiot that the words "drinks a little too much" and "yell" didn't stop me in my tracks.

"What do you mean by 'yell'?"

"I mean that sometimes she drinks too much and will yell in her apartment."

"Um . . . at whom?"

"Nobody in particular."

"How often does this happen?"

"Not very often—every few months. Look, she's a very nice person; she won't bother you. She'll love your animals. I promise."

"OK," I said, trusting a total stranger about another total stranger who was maybe insane. When I hear anything about crazy people doing crazy things that might affect my life, why don't I sprint in the opposite direction? Why, instead, did I start making a story in my head that cast Mabel as this sweet old lady who would enrich our lives and become my best friend?

When I got back to Penny's, I walked across the garden to her place and told her about the apartment. And, small world of Venice, she said she knew Jerry quite well and called him up. The next day he offered us the place. I did have the slightest presence of mind to ask him once again about Mabel. "Really," he said, "you're going to love her." And you know what? I just felt this sigh of relief wash over me: This is all going to work out. This is a new beginning.

Over the last few days Dan was away, I ran around like a madwoman cleaning Penny's place and trying to get everything ready for our move. Our situation seemed to be coming together—except Hopper was a stress case and my body had started to rebel. I wrote to my loved ones back home:

Everyone misses Dan, especially Hoppy who flipped out tonight and ate Penny's gardenia plant. She was very nice about it and, of course, I'm mortified and will have to find her another one. He reminds me of

that moment in Updike's story "Separating" when
Richard and Joan tell their kids they're separating
and their son, John, eats his napkin. Stress can do all
kind of weird things. Usually I feel and look my best
when I'm in this kind of climate, but somehow we got
here and my skin has flipped out with these horrible
cystic pimples. My whole face hurts. So, my skin is
revolting. In both senses of the word.

When Dan's plane finally landed, I'd forgotten about my
skin long enough to be overjoyed he was back. We could now
truly begin the life we'd crossed our country to make: We were
ready at last for California. That night I made guacamole from
avocadoes so fresh they tasted like buttery nuts and lemon
pepper chicken wrapped in warm, fresh corn tortillas from the
Oaxacan market on Venice Boulevard. I made salad and homemade salsa. And I got us some beer. With Dan back, a calm
came over our little cottage in Penny's garden. That night, ready
for our future, we tucked into the little bed under the eaves,
Hopper lying at the end and Ellison purring like mad on Dan's
chest. As we lay there, we listened to our friend the mockingbird, who never wanted us to sleep a wink, chatter and squawk
and yell until we had to put in earplugs so we could drift off, the
windows blowing a light tropical breeze on our faces.

CHAPTER 7

I was standing in a CVS drugstore with Dan trying to figure out which was the best and also the cheapest mop for our new place when it occurred to me that, maybe, just for the heck of it, I should try a pregnancy test. The pimples were still screaming underneath the skin on my cheeks, chin and forehead and I couldn't remember when I was supposed to get my period, but it seemed like it should have happened already. I wasn't very serious about this. I picked up a hot-pink-two-test box and handed it with the mop and a Mounds bar to Dan to pay for while I stood to the side and caught up on gossip in US and People. It is odd, in retrospect, that such a seminal moment as buying my first pregnancy test at age thirty-three was not making a blip on my radar, but even Dan didn't blink. Despite what they teach you in high school health class, I assumed pregnancy was not the easiest thing to achieve in the world, so

I didn't take birth control pills. We just used condoms and the rhythm method because I have a very regular cycle.

When we got home from CVS, we ate our dinner of take-out fish tacos from a place on Main Street in the midst of all our boxes, piled around us like lost friends in our new place. I started working on setting up the bathroom and Dan was putting together the bed frame he'd made the year before out of dark barn wood which he'd shellacked until it shone. Ellison was checking out the patio and Hopper was on my heels everywhere I turned. And then I remembered the pregnancy test. I decided to try it.

I was sitting on the toilet, boxes of bathroom stuff all around me, the tub filled with Bon Ami, when the little window on the wand showed two lines. Huh. Maybe I'd read the box wrong? I picked it up. Two lines means pregnant, it said. This can't be possible. We had only had sex that one night two weeks ago before Dan left. I'm serious—we were just too stressed and too much was going on. I dribbled a little more on a new wand. Again, two lines.

"Uh, Dan? Can you come in here?"

"Sure." He sounded chipper and I could tell he'd forgotten all about CVS and the test.

"Um . . . This thing says . . . we're pregnant."

His reaction was one of benevolent silence. I say benevolent because his face read one thousand words of shock, confusion, anxiety and then, in some corner, near the mouth, exultation.

Finally, after a pause that felt like hours, he asked, "Should I go get another test?"

That's my husband always trying to fix the problem.

"I tried two."

"Are those things always a hundred percent accurate?"

"I have no idea!" I could hear my voice getting squeaky as the message that my life was about to take a bigger turn than I'd bargained for started to filter through my gray matter. "I'm not sure I'm ready for this," I said. I hadn't even been married a year and my career was important to me. I wanted to "make it" or "do something important" first. Having children was something I'd do when everything was settled, when I was finally (it was going to happen, right?) all grown up.

"Just stay here. I'm getting another test." In a flash he was out the door, leaving me stranded on the toilet with the wand that had two very clear blue lines. Hopper and Ellison have never liked closed doors, so as I sat there on the toilet, frozen, my mind rattling in a million directions at once, Hopper hit the door open with his paw and they both came in to join the party. I surveyed them seriously.

"I don't know, guys," I said. "This could get interesting." Dan came home so quickly he must have run the entire way to the drugstore and back. I opened the new box and tried again. Two lines. "Dan, this is really happening."

A smile came across his face, slow and handsome, the same smile that breaks the hearts of all the girls who meet him and, one day, will come across my son's face and make me melt with devotion (but I'm getting ahead of myself). "Wow, baby! We're pregnant."

"Is that OK?" I asked both him and myself at the same time.

"Is that OK? Fuck, man, it's great. I've always wanted a family and it's weird timing and all, but" (here comes the eternal optimist) "we can do this! I mean, thank God something came easily. This is a gift!"

And he reached down, picked me up off the toilet, hugged me as I pulled up my panties and gave me a long, loving kiss. This, in a nutshell, is my husband: He will rise to meet any challenge and be gentle and optimistic about it the whole way in. Sometimes this drives me crazy because it makes me feel like I'm a nut who's mixed up and anxious inside. But, mostly, his gentle ability to think forward and positively keeps me sane and, sometimes, calm.

Although it might seem normal for a couple to celebrate in such a moment by making love, although the impulse was there, we were both unsure if this was advisable to do in the first, deli- cate days of a pregnancy. So, instead, we made some Sleepytime Tea, unpacked a few more boxes and got into bed. We lay there in the dark, incredulous and excited.

CHAPTER 8

A week into carrying this precious news around inside me like a special jewel that only my mother, my father, my stepmother, my brother, my sister-in-law, my friend Vanessa, my friend Jess and, of course, Dan and I knew about, the nausea hit me like a tidal wave. By nausea I'm not talking about something that can be fixed with a few Saltines and some ginger ale. This was full-on dizziness, vomiting, diarrhea, dry heaves, unable-to-move sickness. When I stopped to think, I realized I'd been feeling a little bit nauseous for a while, but I had just assumed it was nerves from moving or the effects of the Mrs. Meyer's Clean Day Smelliest Cleaning Products in the World I'd purchased to wash our new apartment. But suddenly, I was plunged into the rabbit hole of not morning but *all-fucking-day* sickness otherwise known in the medical lingo as "hyperemesis gravidurum." It kept me in bed (when I wasn't dangling over the toilet) for four months. When I tell you this was a major drag, I am understating what it was like to be in a new city and a new apartment with only the bed, the bathroom and the kitchen set up; boxes everywhere; and not being able to move, shower or speak without barfing. Forget working. Running around as a freelancer for public radio was out of the question. I even had to back out of a part-time job I'd taken at a doggie couture store. Dan had to do everything. I really mean *everything*. He had to find jobs, go out on jobs, clean, take Hopper for walks, feed Ellison, make Hopper's food (Hopper has allergies and so we make him twice weekly a huge pot of ground lamb, rice, kale, carrots, apple sauce and flaxseed oil), clean the kitty litter, try to feed me, spend endless hours at the supermarket looking for something I might consider eating, unpack a little bit here and there, navigate a new city, organize our bills—you get the picture. Sometimes Dan called me while he stood flummoxed in the supermarket, overwhelmed by the options and dead sure anything he chose would be wrong. Although laughing made me feel more nauseous, when Dan came home with things like three bags of lemon-drop candies or ten boxes of frozen waffles because I'd choked one down the day before, it made me giggle. He was desperate for me to eat anything, even junk.

But nothing made eating feel like anything less than torture. Nothing homeopathic, natural or even chemical worked. A charming tangential effect of hyperemesis gravidurum is that most of those who suffer from it are also treated to an inordinate amount of mucus production. So, I was also gagging on the mucus running down my throat. I went through three boxes of tissues a day. I was, in short, miserable.

For the first couple of weeks, I kept thinking, "This too will pass; this will lift." It seemed, for a little while, almost laughable that I couldn't even finish a phone call without hanging up to go puke. But then it became my life. I was no longer the captain of my body; I was, instead, the vessel. E-mail became my mode of communication, the bedroom my vista. The undiscovered city outside my walls went on without me; my universe shrank to a few hundred square feet. I felt further isolated because I wasn't sure if I should tell people via the blog about the pregnancy. It was still early and if something were to happen to the baby, unannouncing it publicly seemed like a drag. So, I continued to post, but about anything and everything else I could think of. And I read. Nothing complicated—that would have been too much for my brain, stomach and heart. I decided to start, in earnest, the assignment I had intended to do on our cross-country trip, which was to reread the Little House on the Prairie series. My mother had given it to me for my birthday the year before, a "remembrance of things past" gift. So, in bed, I began again, at the beginning, with *Little House in the Big Woods*, which, like looking through a glass semi-darkly, reminded me of my early life when my parents and Aran and I lived in Gouldsboro in our own little house in the big woods. As I read, I remembered lying in my top bunk bed in some Chinese silk PJs my uncle Jay had bought for me in Boston's Chinatown, and thinking, before I drifted off to sleep, that the lines between Laura, Ma and Pa and my life were not that distinct. I guessed Aran wasn't very much like Mary, though.

I sat in one place, a glass of ginger ale next to me and various plates of foods Dan had made sitting untouched (money down the drain!) on the bedside table. With each page, the experiences of the Ingallses and their journey west opened up to me with the freshness of a first read and the familiarity of coming home to a best childhood friend. What I lacked in new friends and new experiences in a new city I supplanted with the epic story of one family out on the prairie trying not only to survive, but also to define what we have come to understand as American. And, as I read, the Little House books came to define the narrative structure of my life, giving it a form that somehow made sense or, at least, had a beginning, middle and end right there on the pages I held in my hands. When I got to the end of the series and Laura was sick with her first baby, Rose, I felt that, despite her story having happened many years ago and my story happening as I read, we were, once again, kindred spirits in the adult world, too.

There was another wrinkle in our lives on top of the unexpected baby, the puking and Dan having to do all the job hunting and working; in addition to the apartment in boxes and the house still smelling like Mrs. Meyer's Disgusting Flowery Lemon Verbena everywhere I turned even though Dan had tried, diligently, to reclean the fridge and the bathroom with Dr. Bronner's unscented cleaning soap. It was Mabel. Our kind, daffy upstairs neighbor.

Mabel was close to six feet tall, in her late sixties (but looked more like her late seventies), had a gray, wavy, grown-out Joan Jett kind of 'do and always wore the same navy blue sweatpants pushed up on her calves, white Keds and a large, white man's T-shirt with the words VENICE BEACH in colorful puff script emblazoned on the front. She had buried a cat, she told us, in the cactus garden in front of our living room windows. She was proud, she said, of the garden, which she tended regularly in homage to her old friend.

On our second night in our apartment, we'd had our first Mabel episode. I was sitting on the patio talking on the phone with my friend Annette when Mabel started yelling in this strangled madwoman-in-the-attic voice from her apartment, "Shut the fuck up you fucking assholes shut up shut up shut up I'm trying to sleep." It was nine p.m. Dan was cleaning the stove and came running out with an alarmed rooster look on his face and asked me who it was, but before I could answer he went running outside to do who-knows-what. He does this sometimes. Runs in exactly the opposite direction of whatever is happening. The thing was, the streets were silent and I was talking softly outside and, anyway, who's asleep on a Friday at nine p.m.? Annette coached me and then *made* me, after three outbursts and despite how shy I felt, call up, "Mabel, it's Caitlin. Everything's fine. Stop yelling, please." And it worked. For that night. I wrote an e-mail home to everyone about Mabel's yelling that night, assuring them that this was "no biggie" compared to our first place with the homeless situation. I took great pains to describe the apartment and all its potential (once I got out of bed). Annette wrote back:

Send pictures please! Include the crazy lady.

But then Mabel started to become less of a wacky, funny neighbor story and more of a project. She often hovered just outside our door, or in the sun by the post boxes on the front walkway. When Dan left or came home, she wanted to know if we had received the coupons she had left for us for pet food from Centinela Feed & Pet. She wanted to know how Ellison and Hopper were. She wanted to pet Hopper, who was, at best, a little skeptical about this idea.

Throughout May and most of June, while I was busy puking my brains out and the rest of the country was transfixed with the 2008 Democratic presidential primaries, Mabel thought Dan was Obama. The only possible resemblance is that Dan is tall and skinny. Other than that, he's white—which should have been a major dealbreaker—and blond. She came down one night during one of the debates, knocked on the door and told Dan she'd decided to vote for him. "For me?" Dan asked. "Yesssss I cannnnnn!" she slurred and gave him a coy little grin. When Obama won the nomination, she yelled out the window to Dan, who was standing in front of our apartment, "We won!" and gave him the thumbs-up and a big, ecstatic smile. "Hillary's going to secede!" she screeched.

Once, Mabel came down crying and saying she knew that Dan was mad at her "about the neighbors." From the bedroom, where I sat in bed, I heard Dan say in a conciliatory tone, "No, Mabel, I'm not mad at you. What neighbors are you talking about?" She blubbered some more and, although he tried to tell her he didn't know anything about the neighbors, she could not be consoled. It occurs to me now that it was then, when she thought Dan was mad at her, when she accused him like a jilted lover, that things took a turn for the worse.

From then on, her yelling episodes started happening every other day. One weekend she spent most of her waking hours yelling, "Fucking assholes, shut up, I hate you."

Dan made up a song for Mabel to the tune of "Luka," that song by Suzanne Vega. It went like this: "My name is Hopper.

I live on the first floor. I live downstairs from Mabel. I'm sure you've probably heard her before." And then there's Mabel's response: "My name is Mabel. I live on the second floor. I live upstairs from Obama, I'm sure, asshole, you've probably heard me before."

All of this was amusing when Dan was home trying to make me eat waffles. But then he booked a job as a photo assistant for a weekend in Arizona—with me not working, Dan was taking everything anyone offered him. As his departure got closer, I wasn't sure I was laughing anymore. As it was, there were some basic concerns about how I was going to manage, Mabel or no Mabel.

I was sick enough that even taking Hopper out to pee when Dan was working a long day was a major ordeal that involved puking in the bushes and being pretty furious at eucalyptus trees and jasmine. Another gauntlet was the peony garden of hell down the street. The poet Jane Kenyon correctly called peonies "outrageous flowers," and their scent in the moist Los Angeles air was intensified to a dizzying level. "I love peonies," I thought, "I thought I liked eucalyptus and jasmine . . . what's happening to me?" My nose was my enemy. I had the abilities of the entire LAPD bloodhound unit, and every smell was code red. As I'm writing this, with the distance of memory, I wonder: Would it have been flowers anywhere, or was it because we were in a new place and all the smells were different and therefore repulsive to me? I also couldn't handle spices in the kitchen—I could smell them *from the bedroom* ten feet away even though they were all inside plastic containers in the cupboard—so Dan had thrown out our entire spice rack. I couldn't drive past restaurants where anyone was cooking with garlic without heaving. I couldn't stand the smells of people cooking in their apartments or homes around us. I could smell people's breath from across the room like I was French kissing them. Also coffee, the dishwasher (have you ever really smelled your dishwasher?), the drain in the sink, the fridge, the freezer, the laundry room, the garbage pails on street corners.

There were days when Dan was working that I almost didn't move and—the truth of this still makes me grimace—when Hopper slept all day on the couch and peed in his sleep because I couldn't take him out. There were times when just feeding Ellison was a major challenge. There were nights when I made my husband sleep on the very same couch Hopper had peed on (which we'd clean up, of course—thank God for washable IKEA couch parts) because I couldn't stand his breath, which, really, is never bad—he is the sweetest-smelling person—but for some reason everything he ate seemed to just reek from him. Food—food I ate, food other people ate—was my enemy. And this, more than the husband on the couch who, oddly, I sexually longed for as if my nose and libido were split between two different people, was devastating. I love food. I love to cook, eat, read cookbooks, watch food shows, think about food, buy food, try new food. One of the reasons we were so excited to move to L.A. was the food: outdoor markets, Asian, Mexican, Indian, health food, gourmet food trucks, taco carts, fast food, Suzanne Goin's restaurants—L.A. is a great food town. And food is a huge part of my relationship with Dan. When he first came home with me I made him a dinner of baked kale in the oven (just wash the kale and then put it in a big pan, drizzle with good olive oil, and sprinkle with some coarse salt and bake at 400 until crispy) served with polenta mixed with butter and Parmesan. This dinner is simplicity itself and, when you're just starting a new romance, is the perfect, light accompaniment to the feast of discovering each other.

Before he left for Arizona, Dan rented me the entire Masterpiece Theatre series of *The Jewel in the Crown*—an epic story about the English in India, which is full of sex and drama and death and history and is basically a fabulous way to lose yourself while you can't move for three days.

I had a moment, sitting there after Dan left, when I felt profoundly sorry for myself. Because I felt sorry for myself, I went from missing Dan to being mad at him for getting me into this mess (obviously his fault) and from there I went on to a whole anti-male train of thought, which I was, at one time in my life, pre-son, very prone to do. I finally decided to break the silence about my pregnancy—I just couldn't bear feeling gagged—and I wrote in my blog:

> If men got pregnant there'd be an abortion clinic in Home Depot right next to the hammer section. Guys would go in, get the job done, grab a hammer and then go knock the shit out of something.

And then I shed some tears and felt horrible for thinking up mean, funny things like this when we were talking about an innocent child forming in my belly. My friend Catherine, always the one to point out the positive, wrote in:

It seems totally unlikely but most women do survive their first trimesters without killing their husbands or going postal in the neighborhood hardware store. I don't know how this is possible when you can't do anything more exciting than barf and your hormones are going crazy but, hey, mysterious ways, right? Poor you, poor Dan. You'll feel better before too long. And, oh yeah, this is so exciting! —Cath.

I decided to open up *Little House on the Prairie*, which is book two in the series, and spend time there, soothing myself until I could think straight. In the book, the Ingallses are just beginning their journey west, expanding the frontiers of America no matter what the personal cost. I kept thinking, *Why?* In Wisconsin, where the story starts with *Little House in the Big Woods*, the Ingallses had plenty of wildlife around them for food; they had land and family and a sense of place. Yet just as we had, they, too, wanted more. As I lay there, pregnant with my first child, reading the story that first ingrained in me the knowledge that there was a huge, wild world beyond the woods that surrounded my small house, I was amazed that it was almost thirty years later and that I, too, had gone west. Reading these books as an adult I realized that while they were, of course, about Laura, they were also about the love story between Ma and Pa. There were so many times as they traveled west and encountered obstacles that Pa said to Ma, "You'll see! We'll get along somehow." He was right; they always did get along. But not just because he took care of them; they also survived because Ma was brave, often alone with two girls and their dog

Jack in a campsite, or for days on end managing their isolated homesteads. That day, after my snide blog post about men, as I lay in bed reading, it hit me that the love between Ma and Pa and their deep belief in each other was what made it possible for them to persevere. No matter what happened, they had each other. After a while it started to get dark and I knew I needed to heave my body up and take Hopper out, despite all the perilous aspects of the great, wild Los Angeles outdoors. I needed to be brave.

Later, after managing to choke down some frozen waffles and a glass of orange juice, with my animals next to me, I sat down on the couch and popped an episode of *Jewel in the Crown* into the DVD player. I was hoping I could while away time and sickness with the drama of India's fight for independence. It's important to mention here that our apartment was so small that the TV was about three feet from my face, so I didn't need much volume. The opening credits had just ended when there was a knock at the door—well, less of a knock and more of a *thwack*, a loose fist hitting it hard. I knew who it was, but the force of the blow gave me pause. I called out tentatively, "Hello?"

"I need to talk to you." And then another *thwack*.

"Mabel, I'm in my PJs. Can we talk tomorrow?"

"No!" *Thwack!* I opened the door a crack. Her hand pushed in to try to release the door farther, but I held the door in place. "Turn it down, I'm trying to sleep," Mabel said.

"Mabel, it's eight p.m.," I beseeched. "It's really low. I can barely hear it myself and I'm practically sitting on top of the television. I can close my window if you want?"

She stood there panting and red faced, her hand stroking my door.

"Good night, I'm going to close the door now," I said. With a force I didn't expect, she pushed against it. I suddenly needed to push harder. "Mabel, *good night!*" I yelped and shut the door and locked it.

I closed the window, turned the volume even lower and put my show back on. About half an hour later, I was just starting to relax when what I can only describe as a Mabel-quake hit my door. She was screaming, "Shut up you fucking asshole, shut up you bitch!" and was throwing her body against the door while pounding it with her fists. The apartment rattled and a wooden bowl of blood oranges fell off the counter, the fruit bouncing on the terra-cotta tiles and scurrying through the apartment. Ellison disappeared and Hopper stood watching, his lips curled.

This was violent, if only to the door. I felt vulnerable enough being pregnant and alone in a new city. But I ventured, "Mabel, if you don't stop it, I'm calling the cops." She was silent. I heard her shuffle upstairs and slam her door. I called Jerry, our landlord, who always seemed to be in Cabo. He told me that he was "super sorry." Then he told me that he truly believed Mabel was just a nuisance and would not hurt me. He told me he'd talk to her when he got back and that he was sure she would get better.

That night, after checking every lock and firmly closing each window, puking a few times, and crying about how hard my life was, I finally got into bed. I just needed to make it through the night and then through tomorrow and tomorrow night and then Dan would be home.

By the time the June Gloom, the late spring fogginess on the west side of L.A., was over and done with, and the Los

Angeles summer had kicked in, Mabel had become a big enough problem that we had given Jerry notice and he was letting us out of our lease. I was still sick enough to be nauseous constantly but well enough to go to the Santa Monica Swim Center to swim for twenty minutes a day, which, oddly, was the only time I didn't feel sick. It is the most glorious pool I've ever swum in, even if you take into consideration some kids doing cannonballs into the area you're swimming in, the occasional annoying swimmer who can't swim in a straight line and is always bumping into you, or the slightly odd appearance of Diane Keaton, standing on the side of the pool in a full Annie Hall getup—hat, glasses, jacket, pants. The pool is half saltwater there and was so clean and cool against my skin. And since it's an outdoor pool, the sun would hit my shoulders in a dappled rhythm, like a massage. As I swam, my face wet and cool, reveries of my growing baby filled my mind and I forgot about Mabel and the sickness and loved my life. I could imagine, so clearly I almost tasted it, how beautiful our lives could be once I had my baby, once we found a new apartment, and as soon as we could finally, as a family, put down roots and make Los Angeles our home.

M ost of my memory of that time when we were trying to find a new place and move again is blurry. But I have this one lasting image: We're standing in our apartment and there are boxes packed and mess everywhere (even though we still don't know where we're going) and I've just said something about how totally fucked up this all is, and Dan's standing there looking at me, his hair what I call a "dead clam" on top of his head, and he gives me the long look you might give someone who's talking mutiny. He says, "Give it six more months; I promise, this is the last thing. We're going to do great here, and soon. Everyone always says L.A. takes two to three years. Just give it a little more time." Oh, my husband, always believing in the possibility of the future. His hopefulness has inspired me countless times. "OK," I said.

One day, while walking on the canals with Hopper, I found us an apartment. It was a tiny one-bedroom, a few blocks from the Venice Canals, with a little office nook and a shady balcony. It was in one of those 1970s California-style buildings where all the doors face each other across a tree-filled courtyard. We negotiated the rent down to $2,000, a hefty sum, but at this point Dan was making quite a bit on freelance gigs and it seemed doable. Dan moved all of our things in a day and a half, piling loose books into our car, carrying everything we owned up the stairs by himself. At the end, Dan was covered with bruises from wrangling our things up stairs and through doorways but he was relieved we had done it, once again. It was Labor Day, and the city was quiet except for the laughter and smells of barbecues and parties along the canals. That first night we lit candles because the power wasn't on yet, said a few words to what Dylan Thomas calls "the close and holy darkness" and put our hands over my belly to feel the baby Junebugging around in there.

CHAPTER 9

All fall, I craved a Maine Macintosh apple. That cold skin against my lips, the crunch of the first bite and then the burst of juice. I missed woodsmoke and fall leaves, crisp nights and seeing my breath.

Fall in L.A. lacks that combination of back-to-school, leaves-are-falling, let's-get-our-ducks-in-a-row excitement that one feels in a place that has actual seasons, but it is a time when work ramps up in the movie industry and that, in turn, affects everyone from dry cleaners to accountants to lawyers to waitresses. In the fall, people get serious (well, as serious as you can get living in L.A., with the sun shining constantly). And even though it's sixty-five degrees every day, Angelenos and the transplants from places like North Dakota all start wearing North Face jackets (a thing I never really understood: don't they feel ridiculous wearing a down coat when it's hot out?).

When I was at work one day at the doggie couture store, where I'd been lucky enough to get my part-time job back, this guy came in to buy a studded collar for his pug and started telling me about how he used to live down "here" at the beach but that it was too cold for him after Labor Day, so he had moved to the Valley. I asked him where he was from. "Michigan," he said, and pulled his parka closed with a shudder.

As the city got to work, Dan started booking a flurry of jobs, bringing in more money than we'd ever made. One week he was in Wyoming, he was in Italy two weeks later (his first trip to Europe!), then Seattle, then up in the mountains north of L.A., and then over election week he went home to Maine to shoot for Talbots. I voted by myself, my belly a huge and hopeful reminder of the change we all needed. On election night Dan and I stayed on the phone together, separated by nearly four thousand miles, as the polling results poured in and history was made. Outside my window, parties up and down the canals went wild with jubilation. The next morning I wrote in my blog:

Today, despite what seems like an inevitable deep economic recession if not depression, two wars still going on, and our country in true crisis in many ways, everything feels somehow more hopeful, more possible—and if that possibility doesn't directly affect me, it will affect someone, and that makes me glad. In other news, I found out yesterday that I have an umbilical hernia around my belly button. Pregnancy's a bitch.

Although I still had only a few foods I would willingly eat (a warm roll-up of sliced turkey and cheese in a corn tortilla, bread, apples, bananas, kiwis, grapes, orange juice, salad with only oil, salt and lemon, and the occasional yogurt), I loved hearing about the food Dan was eating in far-flung locales. We'd spend long evenings on the phone as he detailed for me every single thing he'd eaten that day—at the ranch in Wyoming he ate barbecued bison and homemade sausages, corn bread stuffing, wild turkey and foraged mushrooms; in Italy he ate gnocchi, tiny langoustines, cheese galore, morels and drank wine; in Seattle he'd had the worst room-service eggs he'd ever tasted and drank buckets of coffee; in Portland, Maine, our friends Joan and Daniel who live on the Western Promenade fed him till he bulged with lamb chops and raw shaved Brussels sprout salad with truffle oil and grated Parmesan, lovely wines and breakfasts of fresh Standard Bakery bread smeared with thick Portland honey.

Three days a week I walked to the dog store, where, my stomach protruding before me, I sold paraphernalia and treats to dogs and their people. Often when it was quiet at the store and someone would come in alone, I'd have peculiar conversations: One woman told me about how she put dungaree underwear on her fixed bichon every night before bed because "it's cleaner." Another woman told me her tragic stories about the dating life in Venice, even though she was the kind of person who, you'd assume, with her long blond hair, perfect figure and great sense of humor (not to mention two adorable Frenchies), should have been catching only winners. Sometimes celebrities came in, wearing dark glasses or baseball hats, hoping to be noticed and not noticed at the same time. I treated everyone the same: with semi-interested deference because, honestly, being pregnant was enough to get worked up about. Everyone, even the celebs, wanted to talk about the baby and my due date; the pregnancy was a ready-made icebreaker. Some days I worked with Ernie, who came on the bus all the way from Gardena. He had tried for months and months to get a job, but with the recession going on, this was the only one he could get. He told me that he felt that the recession combined with his being of Guatemalan descent were like a double hurdle. When we were in the store together, in between sales, we would laugh most of the day. We'd tease each other with nonsense about his love life, my stomach, and funny imaginings of what kind of a mother he thought I'd be. We'd regale each other with stories we'd heard about our regular customers, and we'd swap recipes. Because I was still feeling nauseous, I was super sensitive to people's breath, body odor and perfumes. Whenever Ernie ate garlic (which was every single day), I made him stand at least ten feet away from me because his breath made me gag. He accepted this gamely, saying, "You're a little *loca, chica*, but you're OK." I considered him one of my closest friends in Los Angeles.

Hopper, my best friend, was my ambassador to the canals. I liked to call him "the mayor of the Venice canals" because he wanted to meet everyone, four- and two-footed alike. He found himself a girlfriend named Rose, a black Lab who lived two doors down and would wriggle and yelp whenever she saw him. Because of this love connection, I made friends with Rose's owner, a screenwriter who sat outside on his patio writing every day of the year, a pair of Bose headphones on his head to block the sounds of people walking by. Through Hopper I made friends with other dog owners, too, and people began reaching out. This is something that I think just happens to everyone who's pregnant—community forms as a visceral reaction to supporting the growth of a new member of the species. Suddenly, in less than two months, we had invitations for Thanksgiving and to Christmas parties.

I loved walking around the canals late in the evening, everyone's lives wide open to the passersby. This is the strangest thing, to someone from the conservative Northeast, about people living on the canals—no one has curtains. I would see a retired record producer asleep in his chair by the window with the *Times* spread out over him at eleven a.m. every single day; or Isaiah Washington—yes, the guy from *Grey's Anatomy*—playing with his kids or watching football on a huge flat-screen TV. Dan saw two people having sex on a couch in front of their windows. We saw marital spats going on in full view; one neighbor doing dishes in a black bra and jeans; and another standing in his living room in his boxers, scratching his head. I often felt like I was inside an Edward Hopper painting, the private worlds of strangers and neighbors spread out in front of me, the light pooling on the sidewalks from large sheet-glass windows that illuminated not-so-secret secrets.

Although I wasn't overly fond of being alone so much, especially being pregnant and still sick, the money Dan was earning was nice and the small simplicity of our lives without any big dramas going on was somewhat grounding. And even though we were in a major city and Dan was gone all the time, sometimes

I felt a little like a pioneer, starting out in a new place with small, doable expectations. We began paying down some of our credit card debt from the huge move across the country and were finally able to less painfully manage my health insurance (over $400 a month) and Dan's ($200 a month). With the extra income, in mid-November, we took a weekend babymoon at Bear Mountain. We hoped that we'd get a New Englandy fix of leaves and fall temperatures. Of course, it was sixty-five degrees the whole time we were there. Because of climate change, Big Bear no longer sees the winter temperatures it used to and resorts to snow-making throughout the season to maintain its economy as a winter sports and tourism destination. Still, Angelenos walked around in parkas, hats and gloves while typing furtively on their BlackBerrys, challenged by the elements and the gloves. Pregnant and constantly boiling, I wore a T-shirt.

We'd rented a small cabin, which was more of a falling-down, musty hovel with wall-to-wall carpeting, no forks or knives, slightly suspicious blankets and a great big woodstove that we kept going in the barely cool evenings—roasting ourselves but loving the smell and ambience of burning wood. We walked lots of trails around the reservoir and into the woods and just simply spent time together before the baby came.

Toward the end of my pregnancy, although I was as big as a moose, I was overwhelmed with desire and love for my husband. When he was home, in between shoots, we spent more time loving each other than we'd ever made time for in the past. I don't know now whether it was the impending arrival of a new life or the fact that we were finally getting a little happier in L.A. or because we were more bonded to each other being so far from home—but we felt free in a way we never had before.

The night Dan and I came home from Bear Mountain, we drove through a ring of smoke that encircled the city as the fall fires raged in the mountains and the Santa Ana winds fanned their ferocity. As we parked in front of our apartment, our neighbors came by to tell us to make sure to shut our windows and not to walk outside. The air was singed, a smell I'd come to dread since 9/11 in New York City.

In spite of those sobering smoke signals, I still think of that weekend as one of the sexiest and closest times I've ever had with Dan.

CHAPTER 10

Over the summer, a small Web documentary company had approached us about being a part of a series of webisodes on first pregnancies. The project was funded in part by Pampers. Our payment for participating, eventually, would be a stack of Pampers coupons. Despite the fact that I was, in my pre-baby naïveté, ideologically opposed to Pampers and what I thought of as their environmentally insidious, disposable, perfumed, chlorine-soaked, landfill-horrors diapers, I felt the documentary might be somewhat interesting for us. I liked the director, a woman named Jenny who was in her late forties and lived in Venice with her two daughters and TV-producer husband. Also, I thought it would give Dan and me something to do around the pregnancy that was focused on baby-making and all its details rather than puking and all its details. The shoot dates included lots of interviews not only with us but also with special guests. One guest, for instance, was scheduled to go through our house to decipher whether anything we owned had lead or toxins harmful to a baby (this seemed a helpful, if terrifying, prospect). Jenny wanted me to help write many of the episodes, and I would get a credit. And she and I agreed that my blog (now as much a blog about pregnancy and all its ups and downs as it was about moving west) was going to be given a link on the website. So, thinking it might be somewhat of a career move for me, Dan and I jumped in.

When Dan was home, we found ourselves sitting on our couch, being interviewed about having an unexpected pregnancy many miles from home, trying to tell our story honestly and openly. It was nice to talk politely about things (a makeshift therapy) even if I was on a different side of the microphone from what I was used to. And some of it was fun.

The unlikely production crew was a team of three (basically very nice) guys in their mid-twenties who knew nothing themselves about pregnancy—or even women, really. They spent much of the time looking shocked or amused by the details of pregnancy (You wet your pants?!!! You still want to have sex even though you're as big as a house?) and, frankly, like they'd rather be surfing. Once, the camera guy stood on our couch in his shoes to "get a better angle, dude."

In the end, sometime just before Thanksgiving, the producers came over and told me that Pampers had pulled the plug on our participation in the project. They had watched our tape and felt it was "too raw" and "too honest." They decided to go with another couple named Candy and Ken, who were "liter" (it was spelled like that) and easier for the Pampers audience to access. In other words, an unplanned pregnancy and months of nausea might not sell Pampers. We were both relieved. The logistics of how involved we wanted the crew to be in the birth were starting to get complicated, and I was no longer sure I wanted my baby on camera at all.

By the time Dan left town again to do another job, I had become so swollen I could no longer wear my wedding and engagement rings. Anything on my feet other than Birken-stocks left deep swaths of red marks. The baby had preferences already, like not wanting me to lie on my left side—doing so would encourage a violent kicking episode and leave me out of breath. I felt a little funny about this—I mean, wasn't this my body? If I want to lie on my left side, shouldn't I be able to?

One weekend my dear friend Vanessa flew out from the East Coast and threw me a baby shower with the few friends I'd made in L.A. She said, "I just can't bear the idea of you not having a shower for your first child!" She made a registry and sent ahead huge boxes of hand-me-downs from her three children. She arrived with her five-month-old son and taught me, in three short days, how to change diapers, clip nails, nurse and soothe. For my shower, she made a towering "cake" out of blue and white Huggies. In a picture from my shower, I'm standing next to Vanessa in front of our apartment wearing a wrap dress I borrowed from my friend Andrea, and my belly is so large and low, it extends in front of me like I'm wearing a canoe.

In the weeks before Christmas, as the hot desert winds gave way to near-constant rain, Dan and I bought a car seat and found a used dresser on Craigslist. Dan painted the dresser white and put little royal blue knobs on it. I imagined someday painting animals and birds on its drawers much like the insects my dad had painted on Aran's dresser almost forty years ear-lier. Dan and I took a birth class taught by an Iranian woman who called herself Petal and liked to compare the cervix to a mouth opening and closing, giving all the men in the room the willies. We made the firm decision to try co-sleeping. My OB predicted an early baby, and, even, went so far as to mention December 25 as a possible date (he's Jewish and, in the moment, it seemed to have slipped his mind that that date might mean something to me). So I quipped, "Oh, I always knew I was Mary!" He looked a bit perplexed and then a little frightened, as if maybe he had a religious fanatic on his hands.

As Christmas approached, and still no child in a manger, Dan and I started to feel like every day together was stolen time. Dan drew a Christmas tree on a piece of paper and we hung it from our big glass sliding doors out to the balcony.

Everyone we knew was talking economy and recession; recession and depression; Bernie Madoff, Henry Paulson, and the bailout. People were nervous. We, somehow, weren't because Dan had some work booked for January and a few jobs set up for throughout the spring until May. But we had friends who were in bad shape. One couple who lived around the corner from us and were freelance artists (he a cinematographer and she a writer) had a one-year-old child. The cinematographer had not booked a job since Thanksgiving. They were going into the winter holidays with nothing to look forward to. I said to him, as if I actually knew something, "Just relax, enjoy the holidays; it's going to be fine." Eight months later they had rented their house and moved across the country to Boston for a teaching job he was finally able to get. He'd had it with the anxiety of freelancing in a bum economy. But we figured, how bad can this really get? Could it really get worse? We had been on a roll all fall, so the recession had started to feel far away and less personal than it had felt when we left home nine months earlier. In the news, stories of lost jobs and lost homes were like a cancer—they spread into every life. In California, especially, things were going down the tubes with a shocking alacrity. Somehow the words that I heard on the news had become so abstract that I almost didn't know what any of it meant anymore. What exactly is a recession, anyways, I wanted to know. What's the difference between a recession and a depression? Is it just semantics that some guy in Washington comes up with so that people can feel less freaked out? As young Americans who have not gone through a depression or a war with a draft, who have been given credit cards like candy and consider shopping an entitlement, there was a part of us that assumed things couldn't get too bad, because, well . . . that would be *very* un-American, wouldn't it?

On Christmas Eve, too tired to go to midnight services, Dan and I pulled out an old beat-up Bible that had traveled with me since I was eighteen, across the Atlantic Ocean to Europe, back again, then in and out of every apartment I lived in and into my new marriage and across the country. I opened up the story of Mary and Joseph in the manger and read it out loud to Dan. It was this line that got me, suddenly, unexpectedly: "And she gave birth to her firstborn son and wrapped him in bands of cloth, and laid him in a manger because there was no place for them in the inn." I looked at Dan over the book and my capacious belly, my eyes welling with tears. "All she had was bands of cloth?" I wailed. This story, which for my whole life had been nothing more than a *story* that signified Christmas, became, all of a sudden, deeply personal. I felt, for the first time, the fragility of Mary, her courage, what it was like to be far from home with a new baby. A year later, holding my one-year-old son in my arms, my life having changed more drastically than I ever could have anticipated a year earlier, I would hear the Reverend Rob McCall's Christmas service in a small church back home in Blue Hill, Maine. In it he would tell me what I was already learning:

> *What child is this? None other than our child. Here is the amazing part: If this holy child is our child, then all children are holy. The HIV-positive baby born just after midnight in Los Angeles to a young, unmarried, homeless teenager who has nothing in the world but her new baby, the child born just before dawn under a plastic tarp in a refugee camp in Sudan or Pakistan, the child born in Baghdad while violence rages all around. A savior is born every minute.*

By the time Rob McCall said these words, I felt my child had not only saved me but, also, made me know, intimately, some of the feelings Mary must have had and, more important, how mothers the world over felt. But I'm getting ahead of myself.

On this Christmas in 2008, Dan and I opened our gifts in the morning and called home. Then we made scrambled eggs with mushrooms the way my Meme taught us to, folding the sautéed mushrooms into the pillowy egg mixture as it congeals and letting the whole thing naturally puff in the pan. I whipped up some baking-powder biscuits (page 544 in *The Fannie Farmer Cookbook*—I make them at least once a week to go with breakfast or soups). Then we went for a walk on the beach, stepping carefully over a dead pelican splayed on the sand, its body finally at rest on Venice Beach. We made a big turkey dinner and spent the afternoon and part of the evening watching DVDs of movies being considered for Academy Awards that our neighbor, a voting member, lent us: *Doubt, Frost/Nixon, The Wrestler, Revolutionary Road.*

Our friends Tim and Jess came from Maine for a long weekend to visit Tim's family. They brought, like little jewels from home, some fir-scented beeswax candles, a calendar of woodcuts of Portland and a whiff of our roots. We made big turkey tetrazzinis together (Dan cannot get through the holidays without my making a turkey tetrazzini that is VERY heavy on the gravy, cracked pepper and Parmesan) and we sat around talking about our dreams while eating holiday chocolates late into the night. That's the thing about Tim and Jess, they've always been the friends we dream big with. We all always want to go further, experience life with no limits. When they left at the end of the weekend, we felt so grateful they had come and given us a bit of familiar warmth to round out the holidays.

New Year's Eve arrived, and a year that had included a drive across our huge, challenging country, many moves, a pregnancy, and a historic election ended with our personal tradition of cleaning. Dan and I like to clean on New Year's until everything is fresh and gleaming for the start of a new year. I've always associated a clean slate with the smell of Murphy's Oil Soap. My whole childhood my mother wouldn't wash our floors with anything else, because her mother, Grammar, during *her* childhood, had scrubbed her pumpkin pine floors on her hands and knees with Murphy's once a week. I've always used it, too. A few months later, when Dan and I were on our way home, we stopped in Connecticut and found my mother's old childhood home. Through a window I peered in and saw, for the first time, those floorboards. Standing there, holding my barely three-month-old son, a huge journey back across the country almost behind us, I could almost smell Murphy's Oil Soap and I just knew that Grammar was right there with us, proud of us even when we were wrecks.

On New Year's Day, as we have each year since we've been together, Dan and I made egg rolls and ate them all day long, dipping them into an array of homemade sauces. We love this tradition of cleanliness followed by gluttony. On the second of January, Dan turned thirty and I gave him a remastered copy of his favorite movie, *The Killer of Sheep*.

On January 7, 2009, Grammar's birthday, our son, Matthew, was born. He was bluish pink and had a knot of curly light hair (it looked highlighted!) on top of his face, and when Dan first saw him he shouted, "Oh my God, he looks just like Aran!" "He does?" I asked. And then Dan cut the cord and the nurses whooshed Matthew to the heating table. Dan went over with him and held his little hand and called to me, "Cait, he's beautiful, he's so beautiful!" And then they handed him to me and he nursed for as long as I could hold him, but I was shaking so much from the exhaustion of pushing for almost four hours that I had to hand him to Dan. Dan opened his shirt and laid his naked son on his bare chest. I saw a look of peace and total self-actualization come over Dan like I'd never seen before. I put my head back and closed my eyes for a moment to breathe and make sure this was all real.

We didn't sleep a wink that night. We were too excited. Dan said he wanted to get on top of the hospital and shout "My son is born!" to the whole world. But he didn't. Instead, the nurses brought us some turkey sandwiches and since, like a shade suddenly pulled back to reveal the world outside, my nausea had finally lifted, I ate my first delicious hospital-made turkey sandwich with mayonnaise, mustard and a piece of romaine lettuce. After I finished mine, in one huge gulp, I started eyeing Dan's sandwich which, dutifully, he handed over. I ate that one, too. For hours we watched our son bundled up in the bassinet next to us, his eyes bravely open as he took us in. He never once cried. I held him and hugged him and Dan learned to change his diapers. The next day all we did was call family and friends and e-mail pictures and eat take-out burgers from a restaurant around the corner and drink big cups of a mixture of grape, pineapple, orange and cranberry juice over lots of chipped ice that the nurses made us, and take more pictures. I suddenly understood all that beholding of Jesus that was going on—the magic of it, the animals and wise men all standing at attention. I don't care who your baby is, when they come out of you, all you want to do is stand there and behold the miracle. It's that freaking special.

II

One bright sunny morning, in the
shadow of the steeple;
By the relief office, I saw my people—
As they stood hungry, I stood there wonderin' if
This land was made for you and me?

—"THIS LAND WAS MADE FOR YOU AND ME,"
WOODY GUTHRIE

CHAPTER 11

The last day Dan had had a job was December 20. That day, a Saturday, is seared into my brain because every day after that was counted, noticed, felt.

During the holidays, as I said, before our son was born, in my vast knowledge of all things financial and parental, I had been advising those friends of ours who were worried because they had a baby and no work, that it would get better. L.A. is known for shutting down during the holidays and it's such an unreal place anyway that I couldn't help but think that the silence that seemed to permeate everything was just more La La Land weird-ness. In L.A., where everything is show and money and big cars and lush houses, it was hard to gauge how much trouble our country was in. People shop like it's a sport in L.A., and that sport still seemed to be in extra innings. At the dog store, people were still coming in and buying studded leather collars, three-hundred-dollar beds, doggie bling and gourmet treats.

Also, there's this theme-park mentality to the holidays in L.A. that obscures real life. For example, there are these people on the canals who own two enormous, Swiss-inspired, multigabled houses right next to each other. They are an older, interracial couple who mostly keep to themselves. In the evenings I'd see the husband rowing the canals in an old sweatshirt and ripped sweatpants, listening to Scott Joplin ragtime on a little battery operated tape player, which he propped up in the stern of his boat. The wife always wore neat dungaree shirts over a cotton T-shirt and khakis. At both Halloween and Christmas, they made enormous displays for the neighborhood kids; people came from all over L.A. to see them. At Halloween, it was as if they had bought out a few Hollywood movie prop shops; their lawns displayed skeletons, cadavers and terrifying little boxes that opened up, and everything was electrically powered to move, groan or yawn. Every inch of each house was lit up in orange and black lights, and they made a mazelike haunted house that sent the children squealing through the night. In December, they made a winter fairyland replete with a snowmaking machine that you walked under, and they covered their lawns with reindeer, mice, elves, angels and sleighs. It was beautiful. The rumor was that they used their second house *just* to store the boxes and props for their holiday extravaganzas. I bring them up because Los Angeles, during the holidays, was like their wonderworlds—over-the-top pretending, as if everyone was pining for holidays with real fall leaves or snow somewhere else. Job losses and foreclosures seemed very far away. Walking under that snowmaking machine, the little white flakes of fake snow falling on my head, I could smell roses and mallard shit around the canals and I thought, "This is so much like those emblematic rotting strawberries in Thomas Mann's *Death in Venice*, I can't even handle it!"

After Christmas, as the new year loomed, Dan said, out of the blue, that he was starting to get nervous about the economy, our lives and our futures and that he wanted to apply to graduate school for a master's of fine art in photography. This seemed like an odd choice, given that more school costs more money. But Dan said, "I'm worried this is all going to go up in smoke. We need a future, something that gives us more stability later. With an MFA I can teach and I will be more marketable to clients." At the time I was still thinking, "How bad can things really get that it makes more sense to go into debt when we're already making money in L.A.?" In a white heat, Dan filled out two applications, one for Yale and one for MassArt, two of the top grad programs in the country. We overnighted them. Somehow having done that assuaged Dan's anxiety a little bit. He had done a proactive thing, which, as we all know, can be a good route to take when you feel like you're sinking. Then we went back to holiday stuff for a few more days while L.A. stayed quiet.

When we got through the holidays, we woke up on Dan's birthday, January 2, to the realization that he was thirty and a new year had started. By the time we got to the movies to celebrate (a ritual, every year), we had been thinking about how much we had in the bank in relation to the jobs Dan had lined up. We knew that we'd better be very cautious with our money because although Dan had work booked for between the third week of January and into the middle of May, those jobs alone wouldn't provide enough to carry us through. After we saw *Milk*, we stood outside on the street in front of the Landmark

Theatre in West L.A. and debated whether we could spend a second twenty-five dollars on two more movie tickets. Again, in my incredible financial wisdom, I said, "Look, honey. It's your birthday. We've got a couple thousand in savings, we're OK. This will blow over. Everyone's still in holiday mode. In a week or two, after the baby, you'll be working and it will be great. Let's see a second movie—who knows when we'll ever do a movie double-header again after the baby comes?" So we went and saw *Slumdog Millionaire*, which is such an uplifting movie it can make even the most rank financial anxiety dissipate for an hour or two.

As of January 1, with no baby, we'd started a new year of our health insurance. We'd now have to hit our $2,500 deductible once again before the insurance would pick up any of the costs for the baby's birth. With two calendar years' worth of health insurance during just one pregnancy, we were already in the hole $5,000 for health care on top of $400 a month in monthly premiums, just for me. Beyond that we had a looming $5,000 bill for a night when I was rehydrated in the hospital at the beginning of my pregnancy. Our insurance, for a host of complicated reasons, was not covering that bill. In all, our medical costs were close to $15,000 for one child, before he was even born.

On January 5, Dan found out that the job he had booked for the third week of January had been put on hold. Still, he had jobs lined up for February and into May, so all we needed to do was have the baby and the rest would fall into place. I'd be lying, however, if I didn't say that, on some level, the deeper worry that was permeating the whole country hadn't made inroads through my psyche.

In the hospital the night after Matthew was born, we still

had not slept a wink but were starting to slow down and feel tired from all that sacred beholding and novice nursing going on. It was around eight p.m. and I was holding my son on my chest and had started for a second to doze off. Dan's eyes had grown heavy and he leaned back on the small bench in our room. A drowsy end-of-holiday quietness closed over us. Then, suddenly, we were shaken awake. I looked up and out the window and our building was swinging. Santa Monica was moving below us. Dan sat up and ran out into the hall and I started to get out of bed, holding my son. "It's an earthquake, Cait," Dan ran back in to tell me. "Sit tight; the building is earthquake safe, apparently." And like that, somehow, the elated, safe bubble that had surrounded us since the birth was punctured and an ominous vulnerability that included this child I must, with my life, protect, took over my soul. I looked Dan square in the face, and for reasons I don't entirely understand, said severely, "I want us to get the fuck out of California." This was just one of those things I can say that is stronger than how I really feel, but I relished the power of saying it. Dan shrugged it off saying, "No, you don't. You've just started liking it here! You just started eating again!"

The next day, we left the hospital (which we kept calling "the hotel" because it was so plush, the nurses so helpful) and came home to our animals who, like the animals in the manger in the Jesus story, also wanted to behold our son, their faces earnest and loving and not at all afraid. Before I had my child, people would say to me things like, "When you have your baby, you won't love your animals this much. They'll just become pets." This idea scared me—could my heart be that fickle? That first night I realized, "They were wrong. I love my animals *more.*" And I did. We all piled into the bed together and slept deeply; nothing had changed except the baby was now on the outside of me.

The following day my mother arrived from Maine. She brought with her a piece of a yellow-and-orange crocheted af-ghan my great-grandmother Gingie had made for my parents as a wedding present forty years earlier. My mother had had the remnant, the size of a crib mattress, trimmed with light yellow satin for our son. After she got done with her own beholding, we all tried to settle into being together. There was a period there, during the first day and a half of her visit, with us trying to figure out how to be new parents and the apart-ment in chaos, when my mother worried we didn't want her there. The truth was we didn't know how to have her there and also adjust to this new thing we had no road map for. I looked at Dan after she went back to her hotel the second night and said, "I need this to work. Whatever it takes. I will die if my mother has come all this way, spent all this money and if somehow, for whatever reason, she feels like she's not needed or wanted. How hard could it be for us to just say some-thing kind or grateful? We need to let my mother in."

The next morning, Mom came over with a roll of quarters and started doing laundry (you could not have told us and made us believe how much laundry we would be doing during the first weeks of our son's life). She just took charge. Since she'd arrived she had wanted to help but didn't know exactly what we wanted, and we didn't know what we needed. We all suc-cumbed with the laundry. And then she cooked for us and cleaned and sat with me as I lay in bed recovering, and she held Matty. It hit me all of a sudden that no matter what had hap-

pened in my family, my parents had gotten so much right with
Aran and me. I suddenly understood what a huge job they had,
just being parents, and how much they had cared and worked
at it.

During those days together, caring for my new baby, there
was a vulnerability to my mother I'd never seen—or wanted to
see—before. Sometimes she would offer ideas and memories of
her own parenting, but very delicately and with no judgment,
and then would say, "But that was so long ago now." Something
touched me about how she felt her knowledge of babies was
rusty and that her desire to help was only as good as what she
remembered from over thirty years ago when she lived in the
woods with no electricity or phone and a big garden. Here we
were in Los Angeles, miles and miles away from what she knew,
and there was a tenderness and a grace to the way she took care
of us in the simplest of ways that seared through the gristle of
family hurt and missed opportunities at better communication
and got inside my heart. My mother went out and found her
way to the Pharm (the local pharmacy that sold medical mari-
juana and herbal remedies on Abbott Kinney) to buy me a
packet of herbs for my sore parts, went to the market to get us
fruit, walked Hopper and held our baby. She met our neighbors.
She walked with me when I took Matty out on his maiden voy-
age in the stroller, which she called a "pram." Some level of trust
was being forged between us that we'd never had before. For me,
this brought up an odd combination of feelings because I was
finally a mother—a full-fledged adult in some respects, who
now had to take care of another human being. But also, more
than ever, and perhaps antithetically, I felt like I needed my
mom. And I think, but perhaps I'm stretching it, that, maybe,

my mother needed me to need her, and that was the blueprint for a bridge. The real bridge would eventually become Matty, who, like a strong brick-and-mortar foundation, sealed my mother and me together in a way I never thought possible.

On Obama's inauguration day my mother left. As Dan drove her to the airport, I sat on our little white couch in our tiny apartment, holding Matty wrapped in Gingie's yellow afghan, and watched the TV transmitting our country's historic day. When Pete Seeger appeared with Bruce Springsteen and began singing Woody Guthrie's famous song, I wept. It felt more personal than just an anthem about the promise of what our country was supposed to be. I could feel in those lines, "From California to the New York Island; From the Redwood Forest to the Gulf Stream waters, this land was made for you and me," how far three thousand miles really was and, also, how suddenly vulnerable our small family really was. An emptiness settled inside me, which I could not shake. I knew by then that our lives were hanging in the balance.

CHAPTER 12

On January 21 Dan went to his first day of work since the middle of December—it was a $200 job. That night, an assistant job he had booked for the next full week, which would have made us $1,500, was pushed back once more. The next day it was canceled.

By this point, we were hungover with exhaustion, as any new parents are, but there was an insidious malaise that had started to permeate every waking and sleeping moment—it took up every inch of available breath and got hold of our lives. Dan told me how people he knew were losing work left, right and center. The photography business, he said, depends on advertising budgets. As magazines went under and catalogue companies went in-house to try to stop the hemorrhage of bloated ad campaigns, the trickle-down effect hit us. And because we were freelancers, we weren't eligible for unemployment.

On January 23, the only job Dan had booked for February

was canceled. I remember when he got the call: I was holding two-week-old Matthew, who was sleeping on my shoulder, and standing in the middle of our tiny apartment, my heart racing. I was stunned. "This is really bad, Cait," was all Dan said. And then he started making us dinner. "Want me to do that?" I offered.

"No, let me do it. I need to do something."

That night I looked around our apartment, trying to figure out what we could sell if we had to: Camera gear? Our one laptop? I turned to Dan and said, "I think the only thing we have that's worth anything is my more-than-abundant breast milk. Should we try to sell that?" It was a crazy-making moment, trying to find something, anything, that would save us.

"Cait," Dan said, "our son needs that milk. That's a last resort." In the end, later, when we were about to cross the country again, I gave my frozen breast milk to a woman with an adopted baby. Selling it, when I saw so much need posted all over the mommy Web communities I belonged to, just felt wrong.

The next day Dan started calling every photographer he knew in Los Angeles and on the East Coast. He told everyone that he was willing to be anyone's assistant or anyone's assistant's assistant, he didn't care. He needed a job. Call after call people told him they didn't have anything, that they, too, were having hard times. He called every client he'd ever worked with, and everyone said the same thing: "Advertising budgets are getting slashed. We're going in-house. People are getting laid off." Back in November, when Dan had been home in Maine shooting freelance for his old company, they were on the brink of scoring a couple of new clients and had told him that they thought they could offer him his old job again for slightly more than he was paid before they put him to part-time and we went west. Dan came back to L.A. and, even though it seemed insane to consider when I was nine months pregnant, he called them back with a counteroffer that included our travel back east and a pay increase that would be commensurate with what he was making freelance at that time in L.A. They said no. In January, Dan called them again and offered to come home at our own expense and said he would work part-time or take whatever they had. They had just laid off half their staff; the job was a no go. One morning, after making another round of calls, Dan came out of the small nook we'd made into an office and said, "Cait, it's almost the end of January and the only jobs I have booked right now are a one-day job in April and five days in May."

One of my most charming qualities is that when shit starts to hit the fan I get hysterical. I panic. I get angry. I say things I shouldn't. "You're not trying hard enough," I screeched at Dan. And then like a machine gun I fired in all different directions: "Why didn't we just take that job in November back home?" (Of course, the smart answer to this was that we would have gotten all the way back across the country and the job would have lasted a month.) "Why are you freelancing? We never should have come here. This is chaos. This is a disaster. We're going to sink. I hate California. I never wanted to come here!" I collapsed on the couch in a fetal position, my postpartum belly like an inner tube around me. Dan stood over me, his face frozen in a deer-caught-in-the-headlights look of shocked, impotent defeat and rage. I saw in that instant, the way his shoulders curved, the way he hung his head, the way his eyes bulged, that he was taking every bit of this on the chin and that he felt the enormity of the world was on his shoulders. I could see he thought that he had failed Matty and me. For a guy as ambitious as he is, as hardworking as he is, who worked himself up from nothing, to be presented with sudden, devastating financial collapse—well, it hit a core nerve that couldn't really be made worse by the harsh invectives I unthinkingly hurled. Nor could his heavy heart be assuaged by anything gentle I might say—I knew this. Nonetheless, I got up and put my arms around him. "It's OK," I said. "I'm sorry. We can do this. We're smarter than this. We will figure a way."

Then I got on the phone. I called my producers at NPR and said, "Look, I'm in trouble. I just had my baby and Dan's got nothing. I need work." My longtime arts editor gave me a story on a play at the Geffen Playhouse. The West Coast bureau chief accepted a pitch about restaurants and the recession for later in the spring. The Northeast bureau chief and I talked about what was happening to us, and she suggested an audio diary. My anger had fueled me to the point of outrage—how could America let me down this way? How could America do this to families? Wasn't it just yesterday that we were watching *Sex and the City* and buying "fabulous" lifestyles on maxed-out credit cards? What had changed overnight? I knew in that moment, as I discussed the audio diary with my producer, that if my story was anyone else's story, I was going to hit a nerve. And I was willing to hit it with a sledgehammer. I was sitting at our tiny raw-wood table that I always covered with a clean tablecloth to make it more decent. Our shared laptop was in front of me. I felt tingles go up the back of my neck because I knew that I was going to expose my life in a way that could be emotionally challenging. But I also knew that I wanted to make something from what was happening. When I got off the phone, I looked at

Dan, who sat helpless at the other end of the table, a pile of bills in front of him and the phone in his hand as he went through them one by one asking for extensions and reprieves. For a moment I felt fearful of what I was about to ask. But then I remembered how, just a couple of weeks beforehand, on the day Matty was born, after hours of labor and still no dilation, I was given an epidural and the Pitocin was started. As I waited for the drugs to kick in, I felt, momentarily, scared and weepy. The enormity of what I was trying to do—bring a human being into the world—washed over me. Dan saw my face getting all crumply and small and said, "Just a second," and picked up the phone and called my father. When Dad answered, hoping, I'm sure, to hear that our child was born, Dan said, "Cait needs you," and handed me the phone. My dad was prepared. When I put the phone to my ear, he started reciting Philip Booth's poem "First Lesson." He'd read this poem to me as part of our wedding ceremony, when he gave me away. As I lay in the hospital, miles and miles from home, he shared it once more, perhaps when I needed it most:

> Lie back, daughter, let your head
> be tipped back in the cup of my hand.
> Gently and I will hold you. Spread
> your arms wide, lie out on the stream
> and look high at the gulls. A dead-
> man's-float is face down. You will dive
> and swim soon enough where this tidewater
> ebbs to the sea. Daughter, believe
> me, when you tire on the long thrash
> to your island, lie up, and survive.

As you float now, where I held you
and let go, remember when fear
cramps your heart what I told you:
lie gently and wide to the light-year
stars, lie back, and the sea will hold you.

"Thanks, Daddy," I said, feeling soft and squishy and like I was a little girl again.

"You'll be OK, sweetie."

After Dad hung up, Dan turned up the iPod and within moments, I was relaxed, focused and ready to push through whatever I needed to in order to bring my baby into the world.

So on this day, two weeks later, I thought to myself, "Just don't tire, Cait. Go forward, keep swimming, you can do this and do it well. Be brave, Cait." I said, "Dan. This could be the worst best thing I ever do for us. It will put a spotlight on us in a national way, but it may also save us." I'm not sure why I said it might save us. I thought that if I tapped the right vein of a collective American story, I might get more work. Dan was used to me exposing our lives—he had, after all, married the woman who wrote the relationships and dating column for a local Portland paper which told our entire town many of our adventures. And although I had been told that NPR was canceling at least one show, was putting remaining staff on furlough, was taking fewer pieces from freelancers and that what I would finally make for each was only $525 (only a couple of weeks' worth of groceries and gas), Dan said, "OK. Go for it. I trust you. It doesn't matter how much you make—we need whatever we can get. But I'm sorry you have to work right now." He said that last part because he knew that inside my heart there was a big

part of me that yearned to just focus on our infant for a while—
to have a bit of a maternity leave. But at two and a half weeks
postpartum, my belly still huge, my milk spraying all over the
place, my body sore, I went back to work. I was shy to put myself out in the world in my maternity clothes and not looking
my most attractive, but I kept my chin up because my family
depended on me.

While my mother was visiting us, I had learned something
important about how little clothes matter, even in L.A. A few
days before Mom went home to Maine, we went to El Matador
Beach in Malibu and walked on the soft sand, the large rock
formations looming like a movie set, the water cool and blue
and pelicans dotting the rocks just off the shore. She wore her
binoculars and an old pair of high-waisted brown Levi's and
she had tied a white cotton collared shirt up into a tight bow to
accentuate her small waist. I was holding my child and walking
behind her with Dan. He turned to me and said, "Look," and
pointed at my mother. I looked. And then Dan said, "Those
jeans are so cute." And they were cute, I guess—but that's not
what he meant. What he was saying was that my mother was
real. Here was a woman in her later years, who had flown all the
way across the country to meet her first grandson with every
spare penny she had, and in this fake jungle of L.A. she wore her
clean, pressed, understated clothes and her binoculars and was
carrying her bird book. This was an adventure for her—one
that she was doing with decency, courage and love. From the
perspective of her age, L.A. didn't matter, the people with
their fancy clothes and cars and fake boobs didn't matter.
What mattered was to be there with her daughter and her
grandchild. The forthrightness with which she embodied that

idea almost brought me to my knees with the deep, fragile sense that I loved my mother more than I had ever known and the sudden, painful realization that she would not be around forever.

The day I said "yes" to the first public radio audio diary, Dan started to take on a bulk of the baby care. To say it was hard for him does not do the truth justice. He felt like someone had just come in and cut his legs off at the knees and taken his testicles while they were at it. But also, and this is the wonderful truth, he loved these private moments with our son. He said to me one night, "You know, this is hard for me. But if it weren't for this situation I'd never get this much time with Matthew. And I love being with him." When Dan said this, as Zora Neale Hurston put it, my soul "crawled out from its hiding place." I knew then and there that for better or for worse our marriage was a rock that tethered me and I would do everything to preserve it no matter what happened.

I also knew that Dan was going to do whatever it took to take care of his family, even if that meant staying home all day with a baby. He had no real road map from his own childhood of how to do any of this, and there was no one in his family he'd ever call to ask for advice. Dan had run so fast and far away from his roots and had become so distant from his own family that when our wedding came along, he wasn't sure he could figure a way to assimilate his family into the new family he was making with me. When you've worked that hard to get away from where you came from, it's hard to keep moving forward and also keep a hand on the past. For Dan, it was easiest to just let go. But I felt that if he didn't at least invite his nuclear family to our wedding, he'd one day regret it. I told him that the idea of his mother not being invited was more than I could bear. I cried and I begged, and, finally, they all came: his mother and father, his brother and sister-in-law. Not only that, but Dan's mother made big loaves of her famous white bread, which Dan makes every Christmas and likes to call "white bread white bread"— full of Crisco, white flour and salt, gooey and delicious. She also made peanut-butter-and-chocolate fudge as favors and wrapped the sweet little squares in tissue paper and put them in boxes she'd made that said THE COWBOY AND THE WRITER GET HITCHED! and had a photo of us on the side. This was an act of bravery on her part, to offer to do all this and to come to our wedding in a town she'd never been to, with a family she'd never met, celebrating the union of her estranged son to a woman she'd met only once. And it must have been hard to see her son marrying into a family to whom he was already so close. That wedding weekend, while Dan and I ran around like chickens with our heads cut off, Dan's mother sailed through the events, a huge smile on her face, her heart open and warm to everyone she met.

Sometime later in the story of Dan and me, when the bonds of family became a lifeline, Dan's mother would hold our son and become a part of our lives. And she would become someone he trusted. But we didn't know that then.

CHAPTER 13

When February came and the jobs Dan had lined up for April and May were canceled, he hit the pavement, going to Express and Barnes & Noble, and to restaurants, bars and coffee shops on the West Side. He went to hotels. He went to woodshops, photo stores, art stores, supermarkets, you name it. Nobody was hiring. People were getting laid off. Stores were closing. The toxic combination of an unusually warm fall and winter plus the recession meant that clothing stores hadn't been able to sell inventories of boots, hats and scarves and were hemorrhaging money. The recession was like a poison ivy rash that was oozing and spreading all over everything. Every day another store on Abbott Kinney or Main Street was selling its entire inventory in a blowout 70% off sale. A week later you'd see the same store with GOING OUT OF BUSINESS SALE signs papering the windows.

One night, Dan came home from walking around looking for a job and said he was ashamed and frustrated to be a "poor sap with his hand out" and "the guy who couldn't get a job." He confessed that he would get to the end of a block of stores and restaurants and feel too embarrassed to walk back down the street past every door he'd just knocked on. So, instead, he'd walk behind the buildings back to our car.

As my husband's sense of self was getting squished to nothing, I dove into finishing the radio pieces I'd been assigned, working and nursing, working and nursing. Every night we stayed up late, trying to plan a way out: Dan applied for hundreds of jobs on Craigslist and sent e-mails to everyone he could think of, and I tried to come up with ways we could save money.

One night, feeling totally weakened by the stress, I told Dan I wanted him to fix it. We were sitting in our office nook, me in the chair and him on the floor below me, and for some reason I just felt like I needed my husband to make this go away. When I said that, I saw his face cave in on itself the way a Halloween pumpkin will when it goes soft. "I'm trying to fix it, Cait. But this is way beyond what I can fix with my two hands."

At times a cloudy tension hovered between us. We both knew the problem was not each other but something larger than either of us knew how to name. In some marriages this tension could have reached a level of toxicity from which no one would recover. Luckily, although it was hard and I wasn't particularly my best self during much of this time, we had faith that our vows meant something. That richer or poorer line? That's the one we were testing.

By mid-February, I could tell that Dan, in some ways, was ready to just throw in the towel. He didn't know where to throw it, but a part of him just wanted to give up. I didn't want to give up. I've always been a fourth-quarter player. When the pressure is on, I rise to meet it. I didn't have any idea what would happen to us if we couldn't fight what was happening, so we were going to fight it, plain and simple. I wasn't sure, however, what the hell we were fighting—a recession that looked ominously like a depression? I wanted to try.

The only way I could think of fighting was with work. So, I burrowed in, putting together my audio diary, which would eventually tell more about our lives than even I knew I was capable of sharing right then. Somehow, though, I didn't have the stomach to write my blog. There was a part of me that felt too vulnerable to tell, in the immediate form of a blog, how our lives really were from the inside. I'd set a precedent of spontaneity and honesty in those missives that I was scared of now. Also, with so many people in desperate situations, I didn't want to seem ignorant of how much worse things could be; even though what was happening felt terrible to us, I was watching the news and I saw much more pain. And, finally, writing it all down, when we were in a full-on battle to save our lives—I just didn't have the energy for it.

Instead I poured what was left of my creative energy into what we ate. When I was sick and pregnant, relegated to reading in bed, I had been inspired by how, in *The Long Winter*, when the Ingallses are so desperate for food, over and over again they turn a few old turnips and the end of a bag of beans into dinner;

a small sack of wheat is ground in their coffee mill for bread, which they eat with every single meal; or a lucky package of beef from a neighbor who resorts to killing his oxen becomes "flavoring" for many days' worth of dinners. Time and time again, Ma finds resourceful ways to make their food last and feed her family.

For my family, I somehow whittled our weekly grocery expenses for three meals a day plus food for the animals to just under $100.00, which, when you're trying to eat organic because you're nursing, is a major undertaking. Each week I made all our bread. On Mondays I made a huge pot of lentil soup with green lentils, potatoes, carrots, parsley, garlic, onions and dried bouillon. On Thursdays, I made a huge pot of turkey chili for the rest of the week. I found that turkey chili doesn't actually need that much turkey to make it taste good. We ate the soups for lunch and dinner every day. I started making homemade hummus. We got vegetables from the market—and the cheapest ones, too—no tomatoes, no citrus, no baby greens. Avocados were fifty cents each and were great halved with a little salt and olive oil. A big bag of fresh, tender okra was cheap and filling. I opened our cupboard and tried to turn everything in it into food. A container of baking powder and the end of a bag of old flour gave me ingredients for biscuits; a leftover hunk of chocolate and some sugar and an egg became skillet brownies to help fill us up (and make our lives feel less bleak). I made huge pots of rice that could be fried with eggs for breakfast or reheated for dinner with the soups. I spared nothing. Every tiny bit of garlic, every onion skin, every vegetable peel went into soup stock, which helped make the chili tastier. I had never in my life been this focused on my actual survival. There was a desperation and, also, an adrenaline kick to trying to pull everything together so that we could eat and keep our bodies going. I'd known what it's like to be hungry for lunch or for dinner. But to feel desperate and hungry is another thing entirely. I had never quite felt that before.

Despite being in survival mode and almost, in a weird way, liking the challenge of going to the Santa Monica Co-Op to purchase only the things on my list, it felt lonely. Anywhere you live it's isolating to have no money, but in L.A., when you're standing in line next to Martin Sheen, who's looking awfully blond and tan and is buying a huge cart of luscious organic produce and all you've got is a few saggy bags of measly dry beans, it's humbling. Even so, as I stood in line in my old, hand-me-down, ill-fitting maternity clothes and bought such a small amount of stuff for so little, I was grateful that I had been raised by parents who had taught me "it's what you do with what you got," and that I knew how to bake bread and feed my family on beans. I told myself, "Hold your head high, Cait. If not for yourself, then for everyone else being hit by this recession right now who's trying to keep it together." When the Oscars aired in our little apartment fogged in with defeat and worry, I felt, for the first time in my life, that they may as well have been in China. I was here, in L.A., and the distance from my chair to the Kodak Theatre in Hollywood seemed wider than continents.

By the end of February, no jobs were appearing on the horizon for Dan. What did appear, unexpectedly, was a call from MassArt saying they wanted to interview him. He needed to get to Boston for the interview. We had so little money at that point it seemed almost insane to consider. I called my brother to ask him what he thought we should do and Aran said,

"Dan has to go. This might be your only chance at something better—a way out. See if Dad has some airline miles he can give you." So, we made Dan two days' worth of peanut butter sandwiches and Dan took a red-eye to Boston. As I was driving him to the airport, I told him about this part in *On the Banks of Plum Creek*, when grasshoppers eat the Ingallses' entire wheat crop, the sale of which they were counting on to pay for their new house and keep them alive all winter. Pa decides that the only thing he can do is walk three hundred miles east in old, holey boots to find a job working the crops of another farmer. I said, "Look at that courage—all of them—Ma alone with those girls, Pa walking all that way alone in old boots. We can do whatever this takes, I know we can." With our new baby asleep in the backseat and my face slick, I said, "Knock their socks off, babe." When he came home a day and a half later, exhausted and hungry, he told me he had.

The day after Dan got back from Boston, it was February 28. By then the window of possibility that things could turn around for us in L.A. was closed and we both knew it. We had just enough money left to get through March if we used our security deposit as our rent. Dan called our landlord and leveled with her. She said "OK" and told him that because of the recession we weren't the only tenants who needed to leave. I then called my mother. I didn't know what else to do. I told her we were stuck. I told her I was scared. I said, in one rush of breath, "I've got a new baby who isn't even two months old, we have no money and I feel like every dream I'd ever had is being stomped to death by this huge, unwieldy, nameless, faceless behemoth. I feel like a failure, Mommy. My husband feels like a failure. I'm afraid we're going to end up on the street." My mother just said, simply, "Come home, Cait. I've figured it out. You can stay with me as long as it takes. I'll set up the back part of the house for you so you have some privacy. It will be OK. Just come home."

A little over a month earlier, when I was in the delivery room, in the haze of pushing and breathing, I remember Dan yelping, "Oh my God, baby, I can see his head, he's right there, you can do it, he's amazing, he's beautiful, you're going to love him so much, you can do it, PUSH!" I pushed. There was music playing on the iPod and Matthew came out sometime after Bruce Springsteen and Solomon Burke, after Ryan Adams and Ray LaMontagne and in the middle of Van Morrison and the Chieftains' "Irish Heartbeat":

I'm going back
Going back to my own ones
Come back to talk
Talk a while with my own ones
'Cause the world is so cold
Don't care nothing 'bout your soul
You share with your own ones

When Matty made his entrance during this song, even though we were miles and miles away from home, it was as if he was coming into that world full of gardens and ocean breezes, craggy rocks and tall pine trees, salty Maine humor and cold-weather common sense. And when my mother said, "Come home," it hit a chord for me and I felt, suddenly, like I knew that my only direction now *was* home. That was where we were meant to be.

In every apartment I've ever lived in, I have kept with me two photos of my mother's house. I've always attached them with a big metal art clip so they make a long, thin railroad of mirrored images of the home I have always loved but also felt conflicted about going back to. One photo is a black-and-white taken in winter; the shingles look shiny gray, and you can see the wheelbarrow for hauling wood standing next to the porch with wood piled in it, and the pond is frozen solid. Tall cattails and grasses peek out of the snow in whispery punctuations, and the spruce trees behind the house kneel in deference under the weight of the snow on their boughs. The other photo is in color and is taken in summer, the grass green and lush, the garden overtaking the raised beds. The phlox, planted in between the vegetables, looks like a stampede of white angels marching across the garden. I have often ached for the smells there—wood smoke in winter and freshly cut grass in summer, the pond full of spring peepers in early summer and then lily pads and fat frogs in late summer, the woods fragrant and untouched. Like everywhere, though, suburbia and urban sprawl have crept closer. One summer when I came home to visit from New York City, I found that with my windows open at night I could hear the sound of trucks far off in the distance, and I almost couldn't believe it; at first I thought I'd gone mad. When I deciphered that indeed I was hearing traffic, it felt personal and like an insult. I lay awake, worried about the future of the little patch of earth that had come to mean so much, where our animals were buried and our peach and apple trees had lived, given fruit, died and been replanted.

When my mother told me we could come, I was surprised.

Not because she isn't giving but because I knew that it was a huge favor. My mother is a writer and a person who is used to her quiet routines. She hadn't had a family living with her since I was eighteen, and it never occurred to me that she'd want our chaos in her life. I also knew she was reaching across years of on-again, off-again mother/daughter tension. We had never tried an open-ended time together without a preplanned beginning, middle and end. But she had offered me sanctuary before. When my college boyfriend, whom I had imagined to be the love of my life, broke up with me with such decided alacrity and cruelty that I actually had to lie down on the floor of my small apartment to keep from passing out, my mother invited me to come home for a few days. I went, flying in a small prop plane from Boston to Bar Harbor, Maine. I got out on the dark tarmac covered with early spring snow, where she was waiting for me, wearing a big down coat. She enveloped me in her arms, saying "I'm so sorry" over and over again. When I left to go back to school, she had managed to get a little food into me and had gotten me to sleep at least one night through. Later, thin and depressed, unsure if I could finish the last few months of my senior year, at my mother's urging that we come together as a family, my father drove down to spend a few days with me. He helped me clean up my apartment, he went to classes with me, and, in the early morning hours because I could not sleep, he walked long distances all over the city with me. Once, as we crossed a bridge over the Providence River, we turned to each other at exactly the same moment and said, "This is our *Independence Day* trip." By that we meant that we were like Richard Ford's characters in *Independence Day*, where Frank and his troubled son, Paul, take a weekend to reconnect while visiting the baseball and basketball halls of fame. In all this walking we were finding a way to forge new bonds since the divorce. And my dad was doing his levelheaded best to save me from myself.

This time, on February 28, 2009, I got off the phone with my mother and asked Dan what he thought. I could see a mixture of relief, joy and anxiety cross over his face like cumulus clouds. Finally, he said, "We need to go home and start over, Cait. We have no other choice." There was a part of me that felt so frustrated and angry I wanted to scream. I wanted Dan to tell me that we didn't need to accept my mother's offer just yet, that we could still fight this out. I wanted this to be someone's fault—someone I could touch and see, not a group of CEOs and Washington insiders who flew in private planes and who didn't know I existed. I also, fiercely, wanted this to be surmountable. Where was *our* bailout, I wondered. As I've said before, I like to get scrappy at the end of a game. My poor father, who coached me in basketball during my middle-school years, had to suffer a bemused mixture of embarrassment and pride when, if we were losing, toward the end of a game I would be willing to aggressively foul just about anyone to stop the clock. Sometimes my mouth would get so saucy that, once, during an important final game, I was given a technical and sent to sit on the bench.

Even though I wasn't done fighting, I could see that Dan felt like he was in the ring with Mike Tyson. Dan is thin anyway, but his weight had diminished considerably and his clothes were hanging off him. His shoulders had started to slump and his skin was a mess, erupting into an angry rash of acne. He had started picking one pimple on the side of his jaw and it was now an open sore. He was pale, which he often is because he suffers from a condition called ITP, which basically means he has too few platelets in his blood; this can make him weak when he gets overtired. I knew, just looking at him, that his platelet count was down. Internally and externally he was taking this out on himself. So, when he said we had to go home and start over, I knew he was telling me he didn't have any fight left. And I knew I needed to hear him.

Then, on March 2, things got worse. My neighbor Bethany stopped me on one of my morning walks, the baby in the Moby wrap and the dog pattering next to me. That morning, as on every morning those days, I was already experiencing the kind of low-level anxiety you get when a huge bill or a letter from the IRS arrives, or when you've just simply had too much coffee. Although I was incredibly grateful that my mother had offered us refuge, getting from here to there with a barely two-month-old baby and an apartment full of stuff and a large unopened sack of dashed dreams in tow seemed almost impossible. Bethany said, "Hey, are you guys having a problem with mold?"

"Mold?"

"Yeah, the dark, furry kind? I seem to have it all over my shoes, on my walls, everywhere. . . ."

I came home and said, "Dan, Bethany says there might be mold in our apartment because she has it and she's a nurse— did you know that?—and she says that it's bad for the baby." We started looking. First we opened our closet, which was against the back wall of Bethany's apartment. On the top shelf, I'd folded piles and piles of Vanessa's hand-me-downs for Matty to grow into that reached up to the ceiling of the closet. I had painstakingly made sure each article was washed twice in Seventh Generation Free & Clear laundry soap. I had dried everything dry as a bone and also folded them neatly enough that they would appear ironed when I took them down. These hand-me-downs, which Vanessa had boxed up and mailed with love, were something I felt protective and proprietary about because not only were they going to clothe my brand-new child, but also, considering our financial situation, I knew we needed them desperately. As I started to take the clothes out, I found little black dots all over the onesies and the tiny pairs of pants. Then I pulled down my pre-pregnancy clothes, which were just as neatly folded next to the baby clothes, and as I pawed through, I saw what looked like black furry mold all over the waistbands and belt loops of my designer jeans (I've always been a person who will shop for one really nice item, like a pair of Seven jeans, and then, painstakingly, take care of it until it falls apart). I started breathing heavily. How was this possible? I found a line of mold traveling from the closet toward our bed. In horror, I yelped, "Dan, look!" And he looked. He pulled the bed out and behind our mattress was a forest of what looked to me like fuzzy, spore-making mold. It was all over everything; clinging to the end of our fitted sheet, spoiling our mattress cover, climbing up our curtains that covered the windows behind our bed, peeling out of a crack in the paint.

I sat down and put my face in my hands. Despite our sleeping baby in the living room, Dan started swearing vociferously. And then he turned to me and said, "That's it. We're going home. Now. I'm not cleaning this up and then trying to stay here. We start packing tonight. I'm not budging on this, Cait." I wanted to just sit there in the middle of our chaotic bedroom, on our moldy mattress, surrounded by moldy clothes and what was probably moldy furniture and cry my eyes out. "Cait, I'm going out to get plastic bins. We can wash all the salvageable clothes and start packing them in those." When he came back, I hadn't done much besides cry and nurse Matty. I had managed, however, to call Vince, our six-foot-three built-like-a-tank building manager who liked to corner you and talk your ear off about anything and everything any chance he could get. "Vince," I said, "we're having what seems to be a mold problem. It's bad. I'm worried about it being dangerous to my child. Has there been a problem in this building with mold?"

"Huh, mold. No, can't say I've ever heard anything about mold. I'll come look, though." He took his time even though he was right downstairs talking another tenant's head off about NASCAR. But when he finally arrived, he checked it out. "You know what that is? That's not mold, you see, that's mildew," he informed me. "There's a difference. Mildew is just common stuff, not at all harmful."

I looked at him doubtfully, but what do I know? He sauntered into the bathroom and started looking at the mildew, which darkened the grout around the tiles. I wasn't sure, watching him, if the mildew in our bathroom was the same thing growing out of our closet, but I was quiet as I waited for his assessment. "You know what your problem is? No ventilation. You've got three humans and two animals in here and you're all breathing too much."

"We're breathing too much?"

"Yes. If you all are going to be in here breathing, showering, et cetera, you need the windows open."

"Well, we do open the windows. It's sixty-eight degrees most days. During the winter with all the rain, though, I guess we had them open less. But every day we've had windows open for a good part of the day." Frankly it had been kind of cold in L.A. at night, the way it can get in a damp place when the temperatures hover around fifty degrees. Having all the windows open all night long with a newborn was kind of unrealistic, although we always left our kitchen window ajar.

"I dunno what to tell ya. You're just breathing too much and condensing everything."

"Vince, I'm worried about the baby. This doesn't seem safe to have around him." Somewhere, despite Dan's line in the sand, I was still holding on to the possibility of cleaning up the mold, getting our lives back together and staying.

"Like I always tell my wife, Bonnie, 'You know what the only bigger pain in the ass than a pregnant woman is? It's a new mother.' You're thinkin' too much. It's just mildew. Clean it up and forget about it."

"OK," I said meekly because I was scared of Vince. When I was pregnant I went through a period of having nightmares about him entering our apartment and hurting us or one of the animals. Likely this was just leftover anxiety from Mabel and vulnerable feelings because I was alone so much.

Vince parted with the advice to "Just use bleach," and made his way across the street to his friend Ed's, where he spent the rest of the afternoon standing around in Ed's garage full of free weights and two SUVs, drinking beer and talking about women and cars, the entire conversation percolating irritatingly through my now wide open windows.

Dan got home with bins from Target in the late afternoon. We borrowed a dehumidifier from our neighbor and started, slowly, scrubbing the mattress with a solution of tea-tree oil and OxyClean. After the baby went to sleep in his bassinet in our office nook, we cleaned the walls of the bedroom and bathroom.

That night, we closed the door to the bedroom, where our mattress stood wet and gasping for air, the dehumidifier chugging along and blew up a camping mattress in the living room. Before we went to sleep, we pulled the bassinet next to us. Dan and Hopper slept on the couch while Ellison and I took the mattress. Around us, the apartment was in shambles. A stack of large, clear bins stood by the door and despite our effort to do the dishes and sweep the floor every night, the space felt permanently cramped by disaster. In the middle of the night, I brought Matthew into the bed with me. When I woke in the early morning, Ellison was wedged between the crook of my arm and Matty. She was purring, her own little body holding on to his with her paws in what looked like a human embrace.

The next day I washed a Vesuvian amount of laundry and Dan started pulling apart the closets and shelves, where we found more and more mold. We threw out piles of things that were unsalvageable. Everything else we washed and then rewashed. Our apartment reeked of plastic bins and tea-tree oil. Out of nowhere I started chuckling to myself about how I would describe this to my friends. I hadn't yet told anyone that we were in the middle of yet another crisis, and I wasn't sure how to begin. I sat down to write a dispatch for my blog. Before I posted it, I read it to Dan.

> There must come a point in a person's bad luck story
> when the reader, you, thinks, What's wrong with
> these people?
>   Ah, dear reader, you may have hit that point
> months ago—perhaps when insane Mabel threatened

me when I was pregnant. Or was it when you'd had
enough of my colored descriptions of puking and
wanting to puke? . . . Or maybe around the time I
described my birth in great (although not entire—I
could have said more) detail?

Well, there's more. And, yes, what's wrong with
these people indeed? What was wrong with Job, I guess,
one might ask too. I'm not ninny enough to suggest
that we're having it as bad as Job—I hope it doesn't get
to that point—but I would describe our story as Jobian
(to throw around an Ivy League term), for sure.

First, I will tell you this: We're coming home.
That shall save the suspense and also satisfy readers
like my mother who has always skipped ahead and
read the end of a book long before she deserves to.

As I read, we started chuckling, then Dan began laughing so
hard at the painful truth of everything that was happening to us
that he ended up putting his face on the table, his eyes tearing.

"Wow, it felt good to laugh!" he said later. And it did.

The next few weeks were a blur of laundry and bin-packing
and finishing my first audio diary, which was scheduled to air
at the end of March. In it I had told everything we were going
through—the fear, the anger, the packing, the anticipated trip
home to my mother's. NPR wanted more: I'd been asked to
start in on a second one, too. So, at night, I recorded our conversations about our financial situation and our moving plans.
In those final days, Dan got an interview for a job as a "banquet
coordinator" at the Ritz-Carlton that paid twelve dollars an hour,

and for a second there it looked like maybe that job could change the course of our ship despite the mold and everything else that had fallen apart. But when the Ritz called Dan in for his second interview, they told him they wouldn't be making a decision for six weeks. He came home and said, "Look. I'm not doing this anymore. Really. Twelve dollars an hour won't fix this. I'd have to work over forty hours a week just to make our rent. So I'd need a second job. And until then we have to hang on for six weeks to see if I *maybe* get this job. They told me that they've had an astronomical amount of applicants and that I'm a finalist but I'm still in a pack of twenty. We can't hang on for this. I'm getting us packed and out. Please, Cait. Help me help us leave."

"OK," I said. "I will. I promise."

The hardest thing about those interviews, he said, wasn't auditioning for a menial job that would not make enough money to save us; it was the guests at the Ritz who were drinking cocktails, swimming in the pool, eating dinner and wheeling Louis Vuitton bags. "Those people are totally unaffected by what's happening to the rest of us," he told me. They had made him feel invisible, and it stung.

Vince stopped by one afternoon to reiterate that the mold— he'd checked—was not a building-wide problem and that, in our case, was just mildew. He went into long descriptions of the differences between what we had and what mold was. Despite the appearance of what was on our walls, he said, we just were dealing with some very safe mildew. By this time, I'd spoken with the other tenants, and every neighbor in the complex also seemed to have mold. It seemed to be coming out of cracks in paint and from behind baseboards. One neighbor had a leak in her ceiling and it seemed that the problem was starting there and fanning out. Our next-door neighbors also had a new baby and were anxious about the mold. But it wasn't worth arguing with Vince; we were leaving. He hovered his imposing bulk for a minute in the doorframe, giving us his questionable mold thesis, then he eyed our boxes and said, "So, I hear you're takin' off?"

"Yes," I said, and rushed in with, "We have to move home with my mother. The recession is really bad. We can't make this work with a baby and everything." I thought this would appeal to him since he, too, had kids. Instead his eyes narrowed and he looked at Dan. "You know, I've never had to move in with my mother-in-law. Never would. You just aren't lookin' hard enough. I see tons of Help Wanted signs around."

"Like where?" I asked, pissed but trying to smile and make nice because I still felt a sense of menace whenever Vince was around.

"I know they're always hiring at the supermarket in my neighborhood in Culver City. And I saw a Help Wanted sign at my local coffee shop just yesterday. Let me tell you, there *are* jobs, no matter what the stupid news says."

"Huh," said Dan. "I went over to that supermarket yesterday and was told they aren't hiring. They said they're laying people off."

"Naaah. You're just not looking hard enough, man!"

"Well, maybe so," said Dan, his face reddening. He rocked back on his heels the way he does when he wants to punch someone.

"Fuck you," I wanted to say. "Fuck you and your weird energy. Fuck you for challenging my husband, you who stands around all day and drinks beer and never works. Fuck you for saying the things you said to me about what a pain in the ass a pregnant woman is and, even worse, a woman with a new baby. Fuck you." Instead, I just said, "Well, we'll look into those. Have a nice day." And I edged the door closed.

"All right," he said, still standing there.

"Bye," I said. "Thank you," and I closed the door. When it was shut, Dan muttered in a low whisper, "I want to fucking kill that guy. What an asshole. I want to fucking smash something right now."

"Forget it. Let's keep packing."

"I don't even know what I'd smash, anyway. It's all getting smashed for me."

Something about Dan feeling invisible at the Ritz had wormed its way into my consciousness. I started thinking about all of the ways many of us feel invisible when someone's gesture or comment seems to take our very selves for granted. I realized how many times I'd been going about my life without noticing a person's face or connecting. I made a decision that day to smile at anyone, everyone. I smiled at people sitting in cars next to me at stop signs, I smiled at gardeners blowing leaves and mowing lawns at the houses on the canals, I smiled at nannies, I smiled at hipsters. And even though I felt like shit and that my life was falling apart, this smiling thing made me feel better. I'd see a look of surprise on a person's face from behind their car window or while they raked a lawn, and then a smile would spread across that person's face, slowly. It was infectious.

CHAPTER 14

At five thirty in the morning on March 21 the phone started ringing. It was still dark out. Dan groaned, threw himself on his side and muttered some preverbal incoherencies. Matthew, sleeping between us, mewled. I pulled my eyes open, and, as if I were coming back to earth from what used to be called Pluto, adjusted to the gray-lit room: "Over there, my son's dresser with a changing pad and overhead a mobile of dragonflies; here, next to me, the physical son; across him is my husband; there's Hopper, asleep at the end of the bed, taking up all the room and making my foot go numb because he is using it as a pillow; and there's Ellison between my legs. We are all here. But something is off. Oh yes, the boxes." There were boxes everywhere, half packed, packed, most labeled with my husband's meticulous numbering system that would tell him via a log he made what was in each box, right down to nail clippers and wine keys. The phone stopped ringing and then, after a pause that was more like a sigh, began again. I struggled up and placed my pillows at the edge of the bed to act as a barrier so Matthew wouldn't fall.

I crossed our 650-square-foot apartment in no time, taking the path between boxes to our office nook. The air was damp and cool, the ocean fog hanging like a curtain over Venice Beach. As I reached for our house phone, my cell phone began to ring. I looked at both caller IDs. On the cell was my mother; on the home phone, my uncle Jay. Had something happened? It was almost nine a.m. on the East Coast. I took the call from Mom.

"Mom, what's going on, is everything OK?"

"Caitlin, I just heard your piece. I can't believe this is happening to you. I'm so sorry it's been so hard. The greed of a few—it just makes me want to shriek. This is my family we're talking about."

It took me a moment to catch on. My brain, frankly, was going out my nipples. Exhausted by caring for a newborn, nursing, packing to move across the country, managing my anxiety and just plain surviving, I was not the sharpest I'd ever been. Finally, I understood. My audio diary had aired already on the East Coast. With my mother still on the phone I logged onto the NPR website and saw my piece on the home page. The photograph Dan had taken of us for our wedding announcement was staring back at me, front and center. In black and white, I looked glamorous and intelligent and he looked sensitive and, maybe, slightly cocky. There was a link to my blog. It had already accrued hundreds of hits.

My cell phone started beeping with another call—it was my dad. I told my mother I'd need to call her back.

"Hey, Daddy."

"Hi, sweetie. That was a very brave piece. People around here have been calling all morning. They want to make sure you're OK. Are you OK?"

"Yeah. Hanging in. I don't really have my head screwed on yet. I haven't heard it or anything."

"It's great. You really put yourself out there."

My home phone started ringing. It was a number I didn't recognize. "Daddy, I need to go. I love you."

When I hung up with my father, I ignored the home phone and checked my cell voice mail. My uncle Jay, in Cambridge: "Caitlin, your piece has created a stir on the NPR site. One woman's offering you land in Arizona, some people are offering you money. And others aren't being quite so nice. But . . . check it out." Just as I was hanging up, my cell phone rang and it was my brother, Aran, calling from Mexico City: "Caitlin. The NPR website is going crazy. But you're going to have to have a thick skin, OK? Some of this stuff is mean. It's going to hurt. Right now, especially, when you're down. But use it. Use all of it—the good, the bad and the ugly to tell a larger story about America. Now is the moment you're talking about—OK? And even though this is your story, try to understand you're telling lots of stories. You're on an American journey—and not everyone wants to come along."

Dan appeared in the doorway of our small, doorless office. He was wearing only his underwear and a T-shirt and looked exhausted, pale and thin. He had a purple bruise on his inner right arm from wrestling and lifting boxes. His light blond hair looked almost tawny in the gray light and it was mashed on his head like a smooshed baked potato. He was holding Matthew.

"What's going on?"

"Our piece just aired on NPR and I guess—well, my family seems to think—it's a huge deal."

With him standing behind me, I scrolled down the NPR page and was overwhelmed by the quantity of comments that were already up. I opened up my e-mail and my mailbox was full. People from all over the country had found me through my blog, through my theater company, through—terrifyingly enough—the Internet. Dan, looking over my shoulder, said, "Oh my God."

Let me put this in context: My previous piece for NPR on the writer Terry Tempest Williams, a well-known and important nature writer and environmental activist who attracts crowds of thousands to her readings, received eleven comments, and for me that was a huge day. This diary had closer to fifty comments, and it hadn't even made its way across the country yet.

As I began to read some of the responses, I was stunned by how Americans were reaching out to us. The most touching comments were from people who had mapped our route across the country and were offering us shelter as we went.

When you begin your travels, perhaps a stop in Southern Indiana would be helpful—no cost to you. A place to stay with free meals.—Anne.

———

For the past 23 years I have lived in Flagstaff, Arizona which is a day's drive from Venice Beach. If you need a place to stay overnight, I can offer you my spare bedroom. Traveling with an infant can be

exhausting and expensive. My home is not far from
Interstate #40.—Regina.

We live in Lincoln, Nebraska, which is on I-80, if
on your way east you need a place to stop you would
certainly be welcome to stay overnight with us. We
have a lovely guest bedroom with private bath in our
walkout basement where you could have some space
and a break from your travels. Just let me know if you
are interested.—Gwen

If you need a place to stop in Middle America,
head to Wichita, KS. I might not "know" you, but
middle America is about opening our hearts to those
in need . . . God bless.—Sarah

After reading these letters and many more that poured
love and prayers and stories that echoed ours of pain inflicted
by hard economic times, we were hit by the edge of anguish,
anger, pain, bigotry and frustration that a story like ours can
provoke. Some of the comments were shockingly mean. Men
wrote in to call Dan a wimp, saying they were sorry I had married a guy who couldn't support me. Others wrote that I'm a
whiny brat who leeches off her parents; some said we were
spoiled artists and should get real jobs. One suggested that the
smartest thing we could do is get rid of our pets. We were
deemed people who had no business having a child and then,
oddly, an argument erupted on the NPR site about whether we
had planned our child and whether that made us more or less

responsible. At first I thought it was kind of funny, this name-calling and ludicrous Internet hyperbole. Until I saw Dan's face. And then, the virtual reality of the words hit me like an avalanche. I was stunned that people, and not just *people*, but *NPR listeners* to boot, would hit someone who's so clearly down. For a moment we stood there, the words hanging in the air, and felt exposed with our vulnerable truth. And then I got a letter in my inbox from a guy who had been a CEO of a company until he'd been laid off. With an unexpectedly sick wife and two children to support he had started his own cleaning company and began cleaning offices and homes to get by. Although buying food was often a challenge and he'd been served eviction papers more than once, he said he was starting to come out of the hole. When he heard my piece, he said, he pulled off to the side of the road and wept. He wrote to not only tell me his story but to offer aid:

> Although our situation is severe by many standards, we are doing a little better every day. I am inching ahead, bit by bit, toilet by toilet. I want to reach out and help you and your newborn child. What can we do? Please let us know. I will be following your blog daily.—Dariush.

And, like that, everything that had happened to us, everything mean anyone had written from the safety of their computers, evaporated. I looked at Dan and said, "Wow. America is out there. And it's behind us. We're not alone."

That morning, the sun started to come up over the Venice canals, hot and sticky, burning off the marine layer. The palm trees came into focus and the flowers outside our windows were garish in the sunshine. The mallards on the shores of the ca- nals woke up with a cacophony of chatter. The air felt light and soft, like a caress. In our apartment amid the boxes and mess of packing and mold, our small family of three humans and two animals was quiet for a moment. Like that, Dan and I knew that no matter what happened, we would not let this beat us.

CHAPTER 15

Dan threw himself into apple- and banana-box collecting from local grocery stores and he started packing full-time. The boxes began to mount to the ceiling.

And then, just when it seemed almost pleasantly impossible for anything to get worse, it did. I found Ellison lying under our desk in the office, her chest heaving, her tongue hanging out, her mouth open. Two of our nicknames for Ellison were "Bossy Boots" and "Bossy Button," but lately she hadn't been her usual bossy self, commanding butter as we cooked, trying to jump up on the table to share Dan's sandwiches (an activity she relished), slapping Hopper if he annoyed her, talking our heads off in the morning and shredding the books and magazines on our bedside tables when we didn't respond immediately. We had thought she was stressed by the new baby and the impending move. Then suddenly she couldn't move.

"Oh my God, Dan—Ellison. Oh my God. Oh my God."

I scooped her up in my arms and held her (what I now recognized as) thin, frail body against mine and yelped, "Call Dr. Carlsen." I was out the door in less than ten minutes with Ellison packed inside the same hard case she'd come across the country in. As we drove, I talked. "Ellison," I said, "I'm so sorry about all this moving and the baby and the stress and the chaos of our lives. You deserve better. From right now, I'm going to make it better. We're going to pack up, get across this country and you'll be back in Maine, OK?" I remembered how much she loved our old apartment in Portland, with a yard where she would roll in the dust on a sunny day and chew on blades of grass. The trip west had been an endurance test, which she gamely accepted and when we finally got to L.A., she'd loved Penny's garden. I thought about all the moving and Mabel. I thought about how in the last year, somehow I had stopped looking carefully. The specific had become blurry. I was trying so hard to keep it together, I wasn't focusing. That was my transgression. "Ellison," I said, "just hold on. We can fix this."

I brought her into the vet's waiting room, which was filled with people and dogs and cats. A dark-haired vet tech named Meg came rushing over. She gently took Ellison from me and whisked her away. A few moments later Meg came back out and said, "It's bad. We need to keep her. Her chest is filled with fluid. We need you to go home and try to get some rest. We will call you."

"OK," I said. "But I forgot to say goodbye. May I tell her I love her?" Meg was used to this stuff, people losing the only beings whom they have let see them go to the bathroom, have sex, be terrible assholes and cry their eyes out. Our animals, really, if you think about it, are the most intimate creatures in our lives. So intimate we sometimes take them for granted.

"She'll be OK. Just let us work on her. We already have a catheter in and she's sedated. We'll take care of her. I promise you."

Back in the car, I put my head on the steering wheel for a moment. Then I called Dan. I could barely speak.

He said, "Cait, come home. I know she doesn't want to leave us like this."

A few hours later Dr. Carlsen called to tell me that he had gone into her chest cavity to remove a backwash of liquid surrounding her heart—the result of a faulty valve. She was drowning inside her body and, he said, likely had been for some weeks. He told me that stress exacerbates this problem and that likely the new baby, the boxes—our lives—had all taken a cat who was functioning with a loose valve and turned her into a cat who was dying of this condition. When I went to pick her up, I took Matthew with me. She was brought out to us, looking fragile and so much older than I'd ever seen, her belly shaved, her back thin. My two-month-old son looked into her cage, inhaled and smiled, made a little gurgly sound and reached out his arms to her. His face said not just, "There's *a* cat," but "There's *my* cat." Dr. Carlsen said, "Go home, spend what time you have with her. And get packed. I think I can get you to your mom's. But hurry."

When we got back to our apartment, Dan had made a recovery area in our office with kitty litter and water and Ellison's two beds on the floor. He had laid a blanket over our fluffiest wool rug to make it even cushier, and he'd put down her little canvas placemat that my stepmother had painted of a gray cat sailing on a ship called the S.S. *Ellison*. Dan had put out an array of bowls: tuna, tuna water, some of her favorite flavors of cat food and a little dish with a pat of butter. Dan had also made a Welcome Home sign with a little drawing of my mom's house and then me, him, our son and Hopper all waiting outside to greet her. When my husband does things like this, when he's this sensitive and thoughtful, when I see his heart open like it's been flayed by a sharp knife, I love him so deeply there are almost no words to express it. We let Ellison out of her carrier and she heaved her bedraggled body to the water and put her whole chest in, her front paws and then her face. Hopper, alarmed, tried to lick her and whined. This last, insulting diminishment cut me to the core. This was not the cat I thought I had. She was frail and sick, and it had happened so quickly—as if the pages to a book had just been turned and we were in a strange, unwritten, non-sequential part of our story.

When I first got Ellison I was twenty-one and it was the summer of my junior year in college. That winter I'd broken up with my roommates. I had moved into a suite with some girls I didn't know. I was, at the time, reading Ralph Ellison's *Invisible Man*. Like the protagonist, I was dealing with the pain of realizing that people can be cruel, even dangerous. My loneliness that winter was assuaged by Ellison's novel. Early one morning I had a dream about a gray cat who would come to me and I would name Ellison. I certainly don't think of myself as powerful enough to have dreams that imitate life, so I shrugged it off.

In June, I was in a car accident with my boyfriend, the one

who later broke my heart. It wasn't severe; still, an insurance guy needed to come look at the Pup, my boyfriend's white truck. I was home waiting for him.

At the designated time, I tripped down our winding staircase to the ground floor and meandered in cork-bottomed platforms, cutoff jean shorts and old, faded black T-shirt I'd had since high school over to the parking lot, where I sat on the grass, the blades tickling my bare legs. Just as I sat, the insurance man, a portly, exuberant fellow, pulled up and jumped out. We exchanged pleasantries and I sat back down while he leaned down to look at the Pup. At that moment a dart of a gray furry thing, fluffy and lemur-eared, came at me and jumped into my arms. It threw its paws around my neck in an embrace and held on like a child. Before I even knew exactly what had happened or what creature had attached itself to me, the insurance guy laughed a deep Santa's belly chuckle and said, "Looks like you just got yourself a cat." I pulled one paw away from my neck long enough to look at the little pointy face and huge green eyes; the triangular, almost translucent, ears and said, "I can't have a cat. My boyfriend will kill me if he comes home and finds it here. Don't you think this is someone's kitten?" He let out a big guffaw and said, "Nope, honey. That there is your cat. See any tags on her? Nope, sweetie, looks like she just chose you." He shook his head and laughed a little more. "Shit, I never seen anything like it!"

"This is the cat," I said to myself. "The one from that weird New-Agey vision I had a few months ago." My landlord, a drinker with a huge shock of the reddest hair you've ever seen and a red face to match, happened to be hanging around when I walked back to my apartment, my new cat draped in my arms. He told me he'd seen her before in the parking lot by a restaurant called Al Forno.

"When?" I asked skeptically.

"Last night, when it was raining. She was trying to find a place to hide." If this were true, to get to me that morning she'd walked under a busy highway and across a four-lane intersection and had traversed many busy streets to come rest under the Pup. Needless to say, I kept her.

In the beginning, she never left my side. She'd come in when I went to the bathroom and sit on my lap. She'd sit on the side of the tub when I bathed and swish her tail in the warm, soapy water. She presided over all of the cooking from the top of a wooden box on the counter and waited by the door until I came home, chortling and talking as soon as I walked in. She figured out how to turn door handles. If someone was visiting and happened to be in the bathroom trying to pee or wash their hands, the door would suddenly swing open and the look on people's faces as they sat or stood there, mid-tinkle, Ellison standing in the doorway scolding them for daring to close the door, was priceless. When I was writing my thesis, she'd swing from the back of an old brown cardigan with leather buttons I deemed my "writing sweater" that hung over the back of my chair. She was a force to be reckoned with, bossy and imperious, disdainful of transgressions in etiquette. She was neat and clean as a pin. I thought of her as a Jane Austen character, prim and bespectacled, with a little round bottom and tiny, delicate, white-capped feet. I had all kinds of names for her in addition to "Bossy Button" and "Bossy Boots." I called her "Ladybug," "Boop," "Bubs," "Bubba," "Belle" and "Belly." Later, when Dan came into the picture, he started calling her "Pumpkin" and

"Little Feet," after the Greg Brown song. She answered to all of them. We said she was the smartest person in our family.

That night in Los Angeles, after we'd brought her home from the doctor's office, Ellison stumbled around, drugged and thin. We knew the stress of our packing was bad for her, but as Winston Churchill said, "If you're going through hell, keep going." We had to keep going, and fast. In a moment of incredible kindness, my aunt Sally and uncle Tom, who live in Northern California, offered to fly down to Los Angeles for the weekend to help us. Dan ordered some ABF Pods, which are basically huge canisters with no wheels that get picked up by an eighteen-wheeler and hauled to your destination. We were leaving, for real.

Over the next few days I religiously gave Ellison her medications. She ate little bites of food, struggled less and less when I gave her pills and seemed mildly content. Each night when I got into the tub with our son on my chest for a bedtime soak, Ellison would tiptoe into the steamy bathroom and sit on the toilet seat, her face taking on the countenance of a dear, wizened owl. Then she just stopped eating altogether. That night I sent a letter out to my list and posted it on my blog:

> Dearest and Closest,
> In the middle of the Laura Ingalls Wilder series, at
> the beginning of By the Shores of Silver Lake, Pa starts
> packing up his family—now Laura, Mary, baby
> Carrie, Ma and their dog, Jack, whom they've had for
> all of Laura's years and who walked underneath their
> covered wagon from Wisconsin to the prairies to

Plum Creek, who defended them with Pa against any
number of dangers, who followed Laura and Mary all
over the countryside. Jack takes a look at the wagon
packed with all their things and goes back inside
their dug out house and lies down in his bed. The
next morning he's dead. He just didn't have another
journey in him.

We leave in four days.

And Ellison, I'm afraid, might not have another
journey in her.

By the time Tom and Sally arrived, Ellison was spending
most of her time tucked into some blankets on a platform underneath Matthew's bassinet, purring loudly whenever we came
to her. My uncle Tom is one of the most thoughtful, sensitive
people you'll ever meet. The minute he arrived, Tom went
straight to Ellison. He put his big hands on her small, fragile
body and sat down next to the bottom bunk of the bassinet.
"Hi, Ellison," he said. She looked over her thin shoulder and
purred at him. As we packed, she came out of her den every so
often and sat next to Tom. He patted and talked to her, de-
manding nothing of her. I was not capable of this—every pat,
every hug, I wanted her to hang on.

I kept telling myself, "I'm lucky. I'm not in Afghanistan or
Iraq. I have a family to go home to. Things will be OK." But still,
I couldn't calm down. When Tom and Sally went back to their
hotel to freshen up before dinner, I got in the shower with the
hope that I'd take a moment to recalibrate. As I was getting in,
I somehow managed to slip and fall, my body tumbling out of

the tub save for one leg, which caught at the knee on the metal rail that housed the glass doors. Before I yelled to Dan, naked and broken-feeling, my leg dangling into the tub and my body lying on the floor, I let the water flood over my lower half and I just put my cheek against the cool stone floor and wished for everything to stop. When Dan found me, the floor was covered with water and my knee had already started to turn purple. He carried my naked body to the bed and put me down, covering me with a blanket. He reached down and pulled Ellison out of her hiding place and placed her thin body next to mine. She purred and rolled against my bruised leg. Dan said, "Cait, I'm not sure how long she has." I knew from the look on his face and the way he paused what he wanted to say next, but didn't. He wanted me to remember that Ellison needed me, but more than that, so did my son and our dog and, frankly, so did he. Dan understands the dark places I can go to and, I think, when he found me on the floor like that, he'd been scared. "OK," I said.

The next morning, with Ellison still not eating, I started jiggering with her medication. I didn't have a lot of time to play with, but I wanted to try anything. I got her to eat a little tuna water and a mouthful of "junk" cat food. I went to the local Ralphs and bought every flavor of Sheba, Fancy Feast, 9 Lives, and Friskies that I could put my hands on. I put out bowls of the chunky stuff, the smooth stuff, the greasy stuff, the drier stuff, the smelly stuff, the stuff that smelled like pâté, the stuff that smelled like cheese. She ate no more than a mouthful every six hours. So then I tried cream, butter, yogurt, turkey, chicken, raw beef, cooked beef, fish, shrimp, brewer's yeast mixed in water and more tuna. I was desperate to make something work. Just as when a child gets sick you pay for it, when an animal gets sick you find a way to pay for it. For me there was no difference. Failing at this and losing Ellison without a fight would be worse than continuing to max out our credit cards.

As I tried to find ways to make my cat survive, Sally held Matthew, and Tom and Dan packed the last of our heavy things into the pods. Tom worked up until an hour before his and Sally's flight, then jumped in a cab, sweaty and dirty, and they headed for the airport.

By Monday morning Ellison had eaten one mouthful of food since Saturday. When I called our vet, he prescribed an appetite stimulant. I went and picked it up. I gave her the first dose and felt hopeful. I thought the medication would surely work by evening. If she ate, we'd be OK.

Late at night, the apartment empty save for a few remaining things and pet hair, dust and trash everywhere, we got ready for bed. Dirt and cat litter stuck to the bottoms of our socks and although we tried to make our blow-up bed on the floor clean and neat, it was, in our current state, almost impossible. Next to me, in the bassinet, our son slept. But I could not sleep. Each moment seemed to dive further into an abyss from which there was no relief. Ellison would lie next to me for a minute or two and then get up and move to another room. She couldn't stay still. Dan had always said that when Ellison nestled down between his legs at night, it was the "period" that signified the end of the day. On this night she found no rest in lying down, near or away from us. She began howling. A deep, feral, bone-chilling, inconsolable howl. Every time she got up I would follow her. I tried picking her up and holding her to me, but that just made her more uncomfortable. By the middle of the night I was desperate. I pumped out some breast milk and found a medication syringe. I filled it with what I hoped was my life-giving elixir and held Ellison to me as I tried to force-feed her. She did not protest. The milk ran out of her mouth and down the soft white patch of fur on her chest and dribbled onto her delicate white stocking feet. I brought her into the bed again. She got back up and howled and paced. This went on all night long.

As the first shards of light crept through the front windows of our apartment, I crawled back into the bedroom. "Dan. This is really bad. I need you to wake up. I think we have to make a decision."

Almost in anger Dan threw the covers off him and took off for the bathroom, where Ellison was. I could hear him talking to her, cajoling her to eat, telling her he loved her. After about twenty minutes, which seemed to me like an eternity, he came back in.

"Cait. This is just awful. I can't fucking believe this."

As soon as he said that, I felt sickened to the core. Whenever Dan ratifies a fear I already have, it becomes suddenly true and then I have to really look at it: I was not going to be able to get Ellison home. I had been finally and totally defeated by Los Angeles. When that sunk in, the stench of twenty kinds of cat food souring all over the apartment and Ellison howling in the bathroom, my heart just broke. I looked at my son asleep in his bassinet, so peaceful, his pink perfect lips pursed in that constant nursing expression babies have, his little hands stretched out. I knew I needed to choose life and hold on tight.

I held Ellison to me until the end. And that may, actually, be my final regret in this whole thing, because I didn't look her in the face before we said goodbye. Dan did. He knelt down and kissed her and looked into her eyes. Our son cooed at her and then started to fuss, so Dan took him out of the room, holding me for a second in his gaze as he closed the door. It was just me and the vet and Ellison. I could feel her heart beating through her thin body against my full breasts. And then she was gone.

We made arrangements for her ashes to be sent to us in Maine and, as we were leaving, Dr. Carlsen came out once more and said, "Take all the time you need with this bill. No rush. Get across the country safely to your mom's, Caitlin. I'll send the ashes as soon as we get them." And then, surprisingly, he reached out and hugged us both to him in a gesture of solidarity I will never forget.

We went back to our apartment, cleaned, packed up the car and I took Hopper for one final walk around the canals. A small gray hummingbird flew up to me and hovered, then dove into a flower, then reappeared and hovered again by my ear. Do I believe in such things? Maybe not. But I want to.

That afternoon we piled into the car, which was full to the brim with gear and yet so terribly empty. Dan hung Ellison's last two collars, both frayed from scratching and wear, from our rearview mirror. Before we packed up my jewelry, I had found an old silver chain. I strung on it a recent tag of Ellison's engraved with the address of our last apartment in Portland that she had loved and next to it I strung a small, worn medallion of Saint Francis. This necklace still hangs from my neck today, the two silvery orbs clanking between my breasts. Like dog tags, I don't remove them.

We sat in the car for a moment and tried to catch our breath. This whole adventure west had taken so much from us and in the meanwhile had given us this incredible gift of a baby we adored. The world is always giving and taking, giving and taking. Fragile and shaky, Dan started our car. He drove a block up the road and then pulled over and said to me, "Cait, I can't do this. I'm too tired to get us out of the city tonight." We got as far as Santa Monica and used some money that a friend had sent us for our trip home on a hotel room and dinner. The next day we left California.

III

Well I stumbled in the darkness
I'm lost and alone
though I said I'd go before us
and show the way back home
is there a light up ahead
I can't hold on very long
forgive me pretty baby but
I always take the long way home

—"LONG WAY HOME,"
TOM WAITS

CHAPTER 16

I awoke with a sinking realization that everything that had happened was true: We had left Los Angeles, my beloved cat was dead, we were in a motel in some town in Arizona and the dreams we'd built up for our lives were dashed. I lay on the hard motel bed nursing my son, my eyes full of tears, my chest sore. Dan started slowly packing our things to put them back in the car. He gave me time to take a swim in the hotel pool, the water rushing over me in soothing rivulets. We drove out of the motel to find breakfast, which ended up being a couple of coffees and two Egg McMuffins from McDonald's. We felt bruised and tired, unsure of anything other than each other and our direction: home.

We drove, stopped, nursed, changed a diaper, drove, stopped, nursed. We were crawling across the country, our car teetering with stuff and an overpacked Thule bin on top, but there was a rhythm to our days that we finally succumbed to. In some ways, we needed to be in motion, always arriving, always leaving. Our troubles felt less permanent this way.

We'd also had a lucky break. That Pampers documentary that had decided to feature Candy and Ken had come through with the huge pile of coupons. The irony was that when we agreed to do the documentary, I had told them that I refused to do any kind of product placement with my child by putting a Pampers on him. I was going for something more wholesome, like gDiapers or cloth. Well, all you need is some projectile poop from a newborn, no money, a road trip and a stack of Pampers coupons to make you change your mind. We were saved from having to buy a single diaper for over eight months. And honestly, when it comes down to it, Pampers work great.

Dan had grumpy moments when he could not believe it was taking us so long and that he had to "lug tons of stuff" out of the car every night and put it back the next morning. Once, having hit his limit of schlepping, he said, "You know, I have talents other than lugging shit," and walked out of our hotel room and slammed the door. Another time he told me, "I feel like fucking Pa" from *Little House on the Prairie* with all our worldly possessions tied to the car, our survival on his shoulders. But honestly, it was. We needed Dan's physical strength to carry our things and to drive. I wasn't drinking caffeine (beyond the little bit you get from a cup of decaf) and was still nursing; also, I was nervous. With Rain Man–like repetition and Rain Man–like rhythm I was saying over and over again, "Our lives are chaos, our lives are chaos, our lives are chaos." I couldn't help myself. Our lives felt like *fucking chaos*. Each time, Dan took a moment to painstakingly explain that when I went into this mode it made him feel like there was no air in the car. He said he was doing his best to make sure our lives didn't devolve into further chaos. He'd point out that we were still together, this was still a country we believed in, and we had a child on whom the sun rose and set and a dog whom we loved. I tried to control it, but late at night when I was tired and worried and it was dark and we hadn't found a place to stay; or when I was nursing at truckstops under the sulfur lights with strangers standing around outside our car; or when I woke up startled by the morning light in a new room, a new town, I'd start in again, saying this phrase over and over, "Our lives are chaos, our lives are *fucking* chaos."

Despite the kind offers of shelter from NPR listeners and blog readers, we never made it to any stranger's home, and a freak ice storm prevented us from having coffee with one reader in Arizona, but the encouraging words from Bridget and Will and Gwen and Regina and many others kept us going. Sarah from Kansas, in particular, cheered us on at every leg of the journey, sending us prayers and love. She, too, had a newborn and shared little stories from her life when she wrote. She'd say things like this:

> You're not too far from my neck of the woods, my dear!!! The wind has been blowing like crazy here on the prairie all day today. You will never experience a wind quite like it. Keep plugging along, you will be home before you know it. God bless.—Sarah

Or:

> Hang in there, my dears. I know every day seems to
> drag like a slow moving steel beam on a broken crane
> and the road an endless abyss, but you are that much
> closer than yesterday. You continue to be in our
> prayers for your safety and safe keeping. God bless
> and God Speed. —Sarah

I'd read her notes and those from others aloud to Dan, grateful for such kindness from strangers.

At each milestone in our trip, I'd send a missive home and post it:

> Dearest and Closest,
> . . . According to Dan we have enough diapers to go
> on a safari— . . . . We have outfits for every eventual-
> ity, a bouncy seat, a jungle gym thing with brightly
> colored animals that hang around M. as he bats at
> them (I have no idea what it's called), two comforters
> and two pillows because we learned on our last trip
> never to cross the country expecting to use any
> blankets in hotels, Hopper's bed, Dan's cameras, my
> recording equipment, my jewelry and various other
> odds and ends which are packed ever so tightly into
> our little car. . . . We also have snacks.

The snacks were the thing that put Dan over the edge. As we were leaving Los Angeles, I made one final dash into the Santa Monica Co-Op to get us some sandwiches—and came out with two grocery bags of snacks. We really had no room in the car for two more bags, but I crammed them in around my feet. And although Dan happily scarfed down the fruit leather and nuts and oranges and apples, their presence indicated to him that I had no understanding of how long this trip was going to take if we didn't get our act together. This bickering of Dan's, the complaining of being like Pa, the annoyance about lugging our things, it was his way of letting off steam. There was enough of a good-humored tone underneath his incredulous irritation with his wife that I could tell he was grateful to have something small to complain about. He actually kind of liked feeling like "fucking Pa," he admitted later.

As we whirred along in the time capsule of our car, America rolled past us like an old super-8 movie playing outside our windows: the waves of grain fields and the pinnacles of mountains; suburban big-box sprawl and housing developments; poverty and wealth; animals and humans. Our friend Laura had given us a musical mobile that played "Eine Kleine Nachtmusik" and bits of the *Elvira Madigan* music. As we drove, a wild range of emotions—from defeat to the sweet anticipation of a homecoming, from exhaustion to the excitement of road-tripping—became infused with the tinny, mechanical sounds of toy Mozart.

Most nights at dinnertime we'd pull off the highway and try to find a town to eat in. In Arkansas, we stopped at a local buffet-style restaurant. Inside, as we surveyed the cobbler bar (how amazing to have an entire station devoted to fresh cobblers!), an older man in blue overalls turned around, his bowl full of peach cobbler, and saw me holding Matthew. "Well, hi, Li'l Bit!" he boomed at Matty. And then he laughed this deep, barrel-chested chortle full of such mirth and kindness it brightened the whole rest of our night.

In the evenings, after dinner, we got our son ready for bed in the front seat of the car and played him Greg Brown's "Late Night Radio":

All across Kansas, all across Kansas
in the night
We'll reach Missouri in the dawn's
early light.
My sister and I in the back seat don't
care how far we got to go.
We want to keep rolling, listening to
that late night radio.

When Matthew was finally sleepy, Dan would tuck him into his car seat and we'd cover as many more miles as we could tolerate in the dark. I'd thought that going west was our most American of journeys, but this journey—the going home—was when I felt America reach out to me and beckon me with its long legacy of triumph over adversity. I started to feel, as we made our way east, that the whole reason we'd ever gone west was to come back home. Somewhere in Oklahoma I started reading little bits of a book called *Went to Kansas* by a pioneer who went west with her husband, son and daughter, only to find that their lives were harder than they could bear in Kansas; so they started home. On their return journey, her son died and then so did her husband. Finally, after months on the road, she and her daughter made it home. I read little bits of her story out loud to Dan at night. It was told in diary entries and letters that somehow made us feel a part of a larger story about America. And the pioneer woman's words and courage inspired me to keep telling our story, even when I was tired and just wanted to collapse onto another dingy bed in another dreary motel and shut the world out by watching bad TV. In Memphis I posted a new letter:

> Dearest and Closest,
> Hopper, Dan and M. are all ready to get out of the
> car and get this part over with. I want the journey to
> continue because the uncertainty of the other end
> looms large.

Morning in Memphis opened full of possibility; we hoped to see Graceland in the morning. After we gave Matty a much needed bath, had breakfast and Dan had drunk as much coffee as possible, Dan lugged our belongings down to the car and slowly repacked it. He was shoving things into the back and into the Thule bin, trying to make it all fit, when he realized that, somehow, the bulk had changed or grown. Maybe it was the big laundry bag of dirty clothes we had up in the Thule. Maybe it was the rearrangement of our stuff, or maybe as we got closer to home we were getting sloppier, but the Thule bin would not close. Finally, and although I didn't see it and know this only from Dan's recounting, this is a lasting image of our trip: Dan had to climb on top of our car to sit on the Thule bin to shut it. This was so amusing to the staff of our hotel that they came out onto the sidewalk to watch, making bets about whether Dan could close the bin. Well, he did, because I didn't marry the Deputy for nothing. But there was a moment, Dan says, when he saw all the laughing faces and thought, "Will anyone in my family notice if I just chuck a bunch of this crap?" He didn't, though, because he, like I, felt that every tiny thing we were bringing home needed to come with us—we had already lost too much. And we didn't, thanks to Dan, lose even one sock.

But by the time we piled into the car once more, it was close to noon and we knew we'd never make it to Graceland and still be able to make tracks. Traveling with a baby, a dog and almost no money while towing along everything significant that you own may not be the best way to do sightseeing. We got some deliciously greasy BBQ and gumbo at BB King's Blues Club, ate it sitting in the front seat trading Matthew back and forth from knee to knee, then hit a congested highway where we sat for two hours in traffic listening to Paul Simon's *Graceland* over and over on the stereo. Yes, the irony irritated us. After we got moving, Dan had his first real meltdown somewhere between Memphis and Nashville. I was trying to record some of our road sounds for my next NPR piece, holding the microphone in the car, and the baby started crying. Dan couldn't concentrate enough to drive and felt I was more interested in recording than in soothing Matthew. I just needed a second to put the gear away, which I was doing one-handed while I held a pacifier in the other hand. As any parent knows, while you're driving, the wails of your child are like strychnine fanning

through your veins. Also, I think the whole Graceland deba-
cle had made Dan grumpy: This was the one tourist thing he
really wanted to do on our trip. So he snapped.

By the time we pulled over and Dan went around and un-
buckled Matthew, both Dan and child had calmed down. We
were parked in some odd turnaround, a jungle of wild-seeming
plants and trees tangled around us, and it was getting dark. I
was nursing, when, after a truck slowed down as it passed us
and the man in the driver's seat took a long look, Dan said,
"That's it, Cait. We need to hit the road." And he whisked our
son back into the car seat and got us back on the highway.

Dan told me he was sorry for erupting but that he was getting tired and anxious about making it home. The adrenaline
that had been pushing us along had started to flag, finally, and
was giving way to bone-deep psychic and physical exhaustion.
Dan was mainlining coffee and still wasn't feeling awake. His
body was covered with bruises, most likely because his platelet
count was quite low, and his hands were cracked and chafed
from loading and unloading our things. His beard had begun
to grow in, long and scraggly. He told me that night that he felt
completely alone trying to get us across the country.

I understood, but for me the trip was different. Despite being our family Cassandra, the sadness and defeat I was feeling
was kept at bay by my son and his sweet murmurings. Something lucky had happened to me when I became a mother. For
the first time in my life I knew, unwaveringly, that I could do
this job well. Even when we felt our shabbiest and most terrified, even while Ellison died and I wanted to smash every plate-
glass window on the Venice canals, I was still able to care for
and enjoy Matthew. Some days, I would dress him up in a soft,

hand-me-down, yellow T-shirt and a blue corduroy footed jumper that had a yellow taxicab stitched on the breast and I'd not just take him, but I'd *parade* him through the Pump Station, a haven for pregnant and nursing mothers in Santa Monica. Many of the other nursing moms in the support groups at the Pump Station lived in Santa Monica and were fancier, wealthier, more together than me. But through some kind of unexpected grace I had confidence in being a mother, and the surety that I was good at this one thing surprised me. I didn't move to L.A. to find this out; motherhood had not been in my plans. Becoming a mother just when our lives hit every fan not only changed but also *saved* my life.

As we drove back across our country, I also felt lucky that I loved my husband and still found him attractive, lucky that I loved my dog, lucky that my husband was driving us across America and lugging our things and keeping us safe, lucky that I could go home again. When I told Dan how I was feeling, he softened. He told me he was grateful I still believed in him. We arrived in Nashville in the dark, the city sparkling with tiny white Christmas lights everywhere, even though it was April.

In the late morning, after getting ourselves organized, we had an early lunch of some of the best fried chicken, cornmeal stuffing, fried apples and coleslaw either of us had ever had, and we hit the road again, hoping to make it to Virginia by nightfall. Then in the Cumberland Mountains in central Tennessee, we hit snow with no snow tires. On freezing roads with steep mountain faces, alongside deep ravines and in the company of tractor-trailers, there was a short period of maybe fifteen minutes where the danger of conditions we couldn't control felt palpable. That night I wrote:

. . . There's a vulnerability that happens to you when
you're on the road that's unlike anything else. You're
a stranger. And you're among strangers, many of
whom are not strange to each other. Plus you have all
your precious things in the car with you. In our case
this means our son whose infant vulnerability weighs
heavily on our every movement, our dog and all our
stuff which Dan's packing and unpacking every night
and morning much to his discontent. There's no way
to not feel like a sitting duck in some ways—we're
just such an obvious target—a car packed to the gills,
California plates (I think we might have encouraged
less irritation with Maine tags) . . . And then there's
the problem of stopping to nurse, sometimes late at
night, sometimes in places that at first seem kind of
ok, but then make us uneasy—me pulling out my
breast in the front seat, then later, taking M.'s clothes
and diaper off to change him. Once, in Oklahoma at
an empty gas station, two guys were hanging around
near our car while I tried to change M.'s diaper and
Dan took Hopper out. I couldn't quite bring myself to
take the diaper all the way off—something made me
deeply uncomfortable. I propped up a blanket hoping
they wouldn't see I had a child in the car and then
finally tapped on the window at Dan to come back.
We left and tried to find a new place to stop and
nurse and change M. But everything suddenly felt
threatening. It may not have been, necessarily, but
late at night it's hard to tell. It's weird, when you stop
and think about it, to realize that you feel unsafe in

your own country. But, of course, this is not a new emotion for many people who feel threatened or endangered in their own communities every day—whether because of environmental pollution, drugs, violence, racism or any kind of intolerance.

When we turned off the first exit ramp from the mountain road, we found a brand-spanking-new Super 8 Motel that still smelled like untouched carpets and drapes, and we brought all our things inside. I took Hopper outside, and for the first time in over a year he saw snow. He rolled around in the parking lot and scampered on his leash at my ankles.

After Matthew was soundly asleep, I went across the street from the Super 8 to the one gas station in town to buy Dan some beer. I must have walked around the store about sixteen times until, finally, I asked the cashier, "Um, excuse me, I'm sure I'm missing it. But where do you keep your beer?"

"Sorry, ma'am, this here's a dry town."

When I told Dan the unlucky news, he thought I was playing a cruel joke. Later, watching the Food Network and eating Kraft cheese and Ritz crackers for dinner, Dan and I made chamomile tea in our hot pot while outside our airless, brand-new room, the snow fell in large, wet flakes and the parking lot filled up with cars and U-Hauls, tractor-trailers, and SUVs.

The next morning we started north. We hoped to make it as far as D.C. that night, then on to New York City to our friend Craig's the next day. As we drove, we were hit by snow squalls that came and went, some so thick we had to pull off the road until the visibility improved. Somewhere in the snow, on the road in Virginia, our son's musical mobile broke and we all self-destructed. Dan pulled tools out of the Thule bin, took the mobile apart in the front seat, and tried to make it work. But this plastic machine, which had entertained our son for almost three thousand miles, was gone, and without it we felt lost. When your baby has been lulled by one toy mile after mile and you're in the final days of a very long trip and your nerves are more than frazzled, for that toy to die with just hundreds, not thousands, of miles to go, it feels like a kick in the gut. I dug a pinwheel out of our toy bag and started spinning it for Matthew, singing and stroking his head. It was almost as good. Later that night, when we were snowed in once more, my faithful reader, Sarah from Kansas, wrote in:

> Caitlin,
> It is difficult for me to read this since I feel your pain
> with the infant. My infant has fussed almost the
> entire night. It is so hard for the little ones. Yesterday
> was my first day back at work. My poor baby cried for
> almost 3 hours while I was gone for 5. Your emotions
> must be wearing thin. Hang in there, Sarah.

The next day, outside of Roanoke, we did a quick walk-through of Walmart and of a Babies "R" Us, looking for another mobile, but musical mobiles seemed to have gone by the wayside in toy departments. So, pinwheels and finger puppets it was, all day long, as the Shenandoah Valley rolled out on either side of us—beautiful farmland, fields as big as planets and huge old barns out of Andrew Wyeth paintings. Dan said to me, "I wonder if you had told the farmers building these farms that an interstate would one day cut right through their land what they would have said." Some of these farms, you could have thrown an apple from your car and broken their living room windows.

Pennsylvania gave way to New Jersey and to rushing cars and headlights and beyond that to the gleaming pulse of Manhattan in the distance. I remember feeling a huge rush of nervous excitement come through me as we hit that familiar traffic, the signifier that we were finally on our own turf, so to speak. No more hotels, no more strangers at night, just friends and the final road home.

The traffic and getting us into Manhattan were Dan's final exhausting challenges. And although I'm sure he was eager to have the driving end, on the other side of this was a blank wall that was living at his mother-in-law's as he tried to right our ship. In my blog that night, I wrote something that scared me:

> . . . Yesterday Dan told me that he was concerned
> that this trip might somehow break him. I pressed
> him on what that meant and he said he worried that
> he just might not rebound. That as a man, as a father
> this whole experience—the not working for months,
> the stress of getting us ready to go, Ellison dying, the
> trip with all our stuff that he's had to pack and
> unpack and pack day after day, the endless driving,
> the vigilance to make sure we're all safe—and Dan

has been very vigilant and protective—and the
exhaustion—that he just wasn't sure where he would
be at the other end . . .

W hen my friend Craig came down to meet us on the street
in Manhattan, his eyes almost popped out of his head.
Our car was covered with dirt, dead bugs stuck like a second
skin all over the front, and it was packed to the roof. Out like an
accordion unfolding came a baby, a breast pump, a dog, a few
huge bags, a stray cosmetics bag, some groceries, a bag of dog
food, a box of vitamins, a computer, some recording equipment
and Dan's camera gear. Craig has a small one-bedroom apartment
that he, at the time, was sharing with a cat and, on weekends,
his girlfriend (now wife). He looked at our car and said, "My
God, you *are* the fucking Joads. I thought it was just something
you wrote in your blog for effect. Dan, you know I have blankets—
Dan! Dan! Don't unload those blankets! Dan, put the blankets
back!" Dan had become so used to unpacking everything in
the car every night, he had almost no ability to do triage.

Craig continued to rib us about our things as we piled into
the elevator and made our way to his small one-bedroom, where
we were greeted by Elle, a cat he had found on the street in
Saignon, France. She was just the balm for a kitty-sad heart!
Her little paws flitted and kicked as she danced around Hopper
while he lay at her feet, eager to show her his belly and please
her. Once we had dropped our mountain of stuff on our friend,
Craig got busy ordering us Chinese takeout. Soon we sat
around on the floor encircled by our piles of bags and ate the
savory, greasy, familiar city food out of their plastic takeout

containers and drank good wine. Our son was quietly snoozing in his car seat. In a pause in the conversation, I asked Craig if he thought we were failures. I was nervous about what he might say because, out of all of my friends, Craig's opinion, given with no sugarcoating, has always been extremely important to me.

"Failures? No. I never wanted you to go out there in the first place! But you did, and you tried—hard—to make it work. You didn't fail, Cait, you've just come home. There's a difference." That night, surrounded by his familiar things and appreciating his presence in the next room, we slept. We were almost home.

The next morning a reader whom I'll call "Mary" wrote in:

Caitlin,
As I watched the evening news this evening I wondered where you were on your journey. There were so many destructive tornadoes along your route, but now I know you were ahead of them. You can be most thankful for that! And we are all thankful you have almost arrived home. Soon your new life can begin. Wishing you sweet blessings!—Mary

Also, my dad had written:

Dear Cait,
I'm concerned about Dan.
He needs some rest & he'll be OK.
Love, Dad

I got dressed and walked down the street to my favorite bagel shop, Absolute Bagel, the same store I had often walked to when I lived on Ninety-Sixth Street, between West End and Riverside. I bought us a mess of bagels and cream cheeses and trundled back to Craig's. After breakfast, Dan and I showered and I started to get ready for a meeting: because of my audio diaries, my blog had gotten quite a bit of attention and a few agents in New York had gotten in touch while we were coming across the country. They wanted to meet with me about writing a book. I was excited about this idea, but everything in our lives felt so out of whack that I wasn't too focused on it. I was willing to try, though. I've always been willing to attempt anything, and the idea that right now our story of financial collapse and the journey home might inspire something larger gave me hope. After my shower I pulled on an outfit of a waist-slimming pair of Spanx panties, non-maternity jeans and a ruffled orange shirt—all of which we'd found for cheap in Tennessee at a mall having recession blowout sales. My entire pregnancy, and after, I'd worn the hand-me-downs that people had found on something called Peach Head, which is an L.A.-area networking site for parents, or on Venice Moms, a similar thing for just Venice-area moms. In the beginning when I started getting big and Dan was the only one supporting us, we had so little money that I posted an ad on both websites asking for help. People were gracious enough to donate entire garbage bags of maternity clothes as long as we were willing to go pick them up. Before my pregnancy, when I imagined myself pregnant, I saw an earth mother eating every healthy food in sight, running and exercising, juicing and reveling in my pregnancy. I imagined my life organized, all my ducks in a neat little row.

I imagined nice outfits that showed off my lovely, toned, baby-bump body. Instead I wore other people's well-worn clothes that were often not my style. I sometimes looked shabby, I assume, to the outside world, wearing a pair of beat-up New Balance sneakers I'd bought at a discount store, some hand-me-down sweatpants from Target and a shirt that made me look more like a Thanksgiving turkey than a cute pregnant lady. But there was a silver lining to this non-fancy, not-very-attractive, barfy time in my life: I met lovely, generous women willing to help. When I think of the kindness that came my way from Peach Headers or Venice Mommies, I get tears in my eyes. People gave me clothes, they offered advice, they were thoughtful and kind—and they were all total strangers. If the recession had not happened, if my pregnancy had happened in an organized way that included money and a successful career, I might not have needed or accepted such help. I might never have had the experience of wearing the battle-tested armor of someone else's pregnancy.

However, by the time we were going back across the country, I had no clothes that fit me. My maternity clothes no longer worked: not only because I'd already given birth but because I was beginning to lose the extra weight—magically shedding over a pound a week. Dan suggested we find a corner of a credit card not yet maxed out and pick up a few things. I was nervous about spending any money on myself. But Dan reminded me of my grandmother, Grammar, who shares a birthday with Matthew. Many years ago when Grammar was accepted to Vassar she did not go because she felt her clothes weren't up to par. It was 1929, the year the stock market crashed, and although elegant, her family was poor. Instead she packed a bag and set off to hike Cape Cod, a bundle of Thoreau's maps under her arm. I now intimately understood why she had made this decision. Almost everything I owned that fit was too tight in all the wrong places or ripped. And I was scared to meet agents, or anyone, with what felt like a cloak of hardship emanating from my clothes.

The minute I put on the new pair of stretchy jeans and a new shirt, I felt like I had hit the lottery. It was exciting, like a first prom dress or a wedding dress. I put on lipstick, found a warmish coat we'd taken to L.A., pulled on an old pair of leather boots, and felt, for the first time since my pregnancy, a little bit like my old self. Dan put Matthew in the BabyBjörn, and he and Hopper walked me to the subway. Before I went down the stairs, Dan grabbed me, kissed me and said, "I'm proud of you. You look beautiful. You can do this!" Then I trundled down the stairs and off they went to Riverside Park.

By the time my meetings were over, I was a little overwhelmed; I suddenly had three offers of representation to choose from. In a way, I didn't even know where to begin. That night, when we left Manhattan to continue north, I decided I'd just sit on everything and see how I felt as our lives shook out.

When we hit Massachusetts on our way to Boston, where our friends Annette and Erik waited for us with a dinner of steak, salad and wine, Hopper stood up in the backseat and started to whine. He stuck his huge blackberry nose out the window and took a long, frosty inhale from the cold spring air. "Now he gets it," I said. "He knows where we're going."

The next morning we packed up once again and, armed with coffees, made the final push to cross into Maine, reading the sign MAINE: THE WAY LIFE SHOULD BE with cheeky gratefulness as we crossed the border. I said aloud, "God's country, as my mother has always said," and we let that thought hang in the air. We opened all the windows to let in pine tree air and wet, cold spring breezes. I wrote of Hopper:

> . . . By the time we hit Maine this afternoon, he was an entirely different dog: His eyes were bright, he wanted to sniff at the window, he was bouncing up and down to look out, then over to poor M. for a French kissing session that verged on such passion it seemed indecent to watch, then a paw knocking at my elbow from the back seat, then over to the window again. We stopped in Scarborough to let him out to run at Ferry Beach. And this, to watch, was like exonerating the falsely accused—there was such grateful, beautiful, heartrending joy to be out of the car, at this beautiful beach, splashing and playing in the clear water and rolling in the clean sand—this made all those days of the long slog worth it . . .

For Dan and me, driving into Maine was imbued with a mixture of relief and exhaustion. When I asked Dan if he wanted me to drive the final leg of our journey into Portland, he said, "No. For one, I don't trust your driving and, for two, I drove us out, I want to drive us back in." (For the record, I'm an excellent driver.)

Later, Dan would tell me that our tires were so bald that he had checked them at every gas station along the way and was terrified we'd lose one. Later, he would tell me that he had been afraid that if Ellison had come with us he might have had to kill her himself somewhere in the desert and he had been planning how. Later, he would tell me that holding on to his belief that he was doing the right thing for us was one of the biggest efforts of his life.

That night, in Portland, we pulled into a hotel. Although friends had offered us shelter, this was our last night alone together on the road, just the four of us. A different kind of journey was about to begin.

So we parked and unpacked our gear for one final night, and Dan sat on the floor, pulled out three folders of receipts and a calculator, and did our taxes, which were due the next day. That night, watching the back of his neck bent over the papers, the soft place in between his skull and his shoulders so vulnerable and delicate, my heart unfurled. When he was done with the taxes, he got into bed, our son curled between us. Over the pillows, I held his big, rough hand in mine and told him I loved him. I knew that for him the days to come were fraught with fear but that what also surged within and between us, like body heat, was deep relief that home again, home again, we were home.

IV

Home, where my thought's escaping
Home, where my music's playing
Home...

—"HOMEWARD BOUND,"
SIMON & GARFUNKEL

CHAPTER 17

When we pulled into my father's driveway, Hopper sprang up in the backseat and stuck his nose out the window. My dad, who had seen our headlights coming ahead of us, was standing outside, waiting. He was holding a beer, and as soon as Dan got out of the car, Dad handed it to him, saying, "Thank you for getting everyone here safely. I know what you've been through, but it's so great to have you all home." Inside, my stepmother, Gail, had made a haddock dinner of filets stuffed with wild rice and sweet potatoes. We ate with gusto, our first familiar food in over eleven days. And then we got back in the car and drove the final twenty miles or so to my mother's.

I was nervous. I had always harshly judged the people who couldn't hack it in the outside world and ended up home with their families. I thought they were losers. I know Dan, too, always thought that coming home to Maine signified failure.

He'd done this trip once before when he left San Francisco and had to cross the country on a Greyhound bus. Maybe it's the insularity of Maine or the hardship one endures in the winter that one can wear as a badge but also feel suffocated by; maybe it's that Maine can at times seem outrageously easy to live in because it's so damn beautiful that it's hard to ever leave; maybe it's because people from Maine can only be from one place in the end, no matter where their lives take them— Maine is that specific. I don't know. But we had believed that if we didn't leave, we'd never make it in the larger world. Maybe this is true anywhere in America; you're always beckoned by the highway out. So, on this final leg to my mother's, although I was filled with gratitude that we had a place to go, I was also feeling fear that we might have to live with her forever. I kept saying to Dan, "I only want to be here for two months, no longer. I want us to get our lives together, fast." Poor Dan! We weren't even done with the driving part and I was already on to the next thing, trying to put parameters on what I should have known by then was beyond my control. I wanted the recession to be over and for our lives to somehow magically transform themselves into success, with Hollywood-movie timing. I wanted my dreams to come back into some form that I recognized. What I wanted and needed were two totally different things.

When we turned into my mother's driveway, there was still snow on the ground. Our thin tires slipped over a frost heave and veered toward a tree. It was very dark, but a substantial sliver of moon shone brightly like a penlight in a tent. We drove up the winding drive, the trees hugging the sides of the dirt and finally came to a halt next to my mother's car. She had left a single golden light on over the porch. It was late.

We unpacked a few basic things. A lamp came on in my mother's bedroom. As we walked toward the house, the door opened and she came out, standing barefoot on the porch in her white nightgown. "Welcome home, guys," she said. "You did it. Come here, let me hug you." She put her arms around us, hugging Dan and me at once, and led us through the small kitchen, then through the open dining and living rooms and into the library where she had set up our room. She hung back, almost shy, as if she was worried we might reject what she had done for us. But we felt the opposite: so grateful to see the care she had put into what she had prepared for us. We almost got down on our knees and wept.

Mom had removed the dictionary stand and my grandmother's desk, the lamps and the big cushions piled on the floor, and had replaced those pieces with my old spindle bed from my childhood and two tables, which she'd placed on either side of the bed. She had covered the tables with photos—of me as a child, of Ellison and of our wedding. On a shelf she had put a needlepoint doll my grandmother had made for me when I was born with my name on it and birth date and also some of my old stuffed animals. The bed in the loft was made with a clean comforter cover and big pillows. Outside the trees hung close to the house like soldiers guarding our enclave. Dan took our tiny son out of his car seat and nestled him into my childhood bed. After saying good night, I brushed my teeth and got in, too, and, because there wasn't enough room in the bed for all three of us, Dan tiptoed up the stairs to the loft.

In the dark, I lay there. I was home. I had made an epic—to my life—journey across America in eleven days. I had lost my cat. I had a child. My husband and dog were still with me. I was at my mother's, where I had never wanted to end up for more than a visit. I had no idea how long we'd be there. I was tired. I was anxious. I was grateful. What had happened to us? It was almost too much to grasp. My life as I knew it had collapsed and something else was beginning. I just had no idea what it was or if I'd even recognize what was before me as my life.

The next morning was Easter.

I sat up, tired from a night awake in the dark staring at the moon and stars through the skylight above me, the white pines tickling the glass, my son breathing next to me, his little chest rising and falling under Gingie's yellow afghan. In the early stillness, I remembered that when my parents split apart and I was living in Paris, I had succumbed to a depression that led to more partying than any eighteen-year-old had any business doing. I stopped going to classes at the Sorbonne and skipped my finals. And I started to self-destruct. My brother was in his senior year in college, about to graduate, and was awaiting the inevitable weekend when his broken family would arrive to celebrate his achievement. This could not have been an easy time for him. But he called me and said this: "Cait, don't forget to laugh. Just because this is going on doesn't mean you can't smile and have fun. Enjoy your last months in Paris; you may never go back." This was a revelation, this permission my brother gave me to have fun. I can't say I did exactly what my brother told me to do. I was still pretty morose and wrote hateful letters to my father from smoky cafés and had horrible nightmares that something terrible would happen to my mother. But I was in Paris, so, honestly, how could I not appreciate beauty? How could I not laugh with joy over a perfect piece of Roquefort spread on a baguette with a glass of Bordeaux?

When I came home, my brother met me at the airport in Boston and handed me a tape of songs by Bill Morrissey and Greg Brown and instructed me to listen right then and there on my Walkman to a song about how a divorce didn't need to be cruel. I walked around Cambridge that week during the festivities, listening to that song over and over again as I tried to understand why my parents' marriage had ended. Over the weekend my mother and I slept on the floor in my brother's suite. My brother stayed out late partying, maybe burning off some of the ether of tension that surrounded our family's every waking moment. Listening to the sounds of college outside on the green, anticipating starting college myself that fall, I tried to think of things I could say or do to make my family fit back together. This was a fruitless effort, of course; the journey we had begun years earlier was in its final stages and we needed to go through this fire to come to who we wound up becoming.

"Cait, don't forget to laugh."

Now it was Easter morning 2009. I was in my childhood bed in the library of my mother's house remembering when my brother had told me to find joy. I've always loved Easter. I love the slushy brown dirtiness of earth starting to regenerate to spring; I love that Easter is not as encompassing and draining as Christmas and only involves a few presents in a basket with grass in it (or, in our family, fresh, damp moss collected from the woods outside). I love that the presents are brought by a bunny. And I love the focus on brunch, one of my favorite meals. So I got up and tiptoed to the bottom of the ladder beneath where Dan was sleeping and whispered up, "Honey?" I wasn't sure if he'd hear me, but it turned out that, tired as he was, he also was awake. "Happy Easter. I'm going to make some coffee. Can you listen for Matty?"

"Happy Easter, babe. Sure. I'll listen."

I opened the library door and stepped out of my reentry crisis and into the living room at my mother's. As if in a time warp, a period of our lives redolent of things past but brimming with things to come began.

My mother had put out Easter baskets for Dan and me and filled them with oranges, pears, a coconut each and some new socks. I made coffee and she came down and we started making a big breakfast of eggs and homemade scones and fruit from our baskets. Bleary-eyed, Dan appeared in the kitchen with Matthew, whom he'd dressed in a little white sweater with Beatrix Potter bunny-rabbit buttons I had found at a thrift store. My mother gave Matty his first Easter bunny. It was amazing to see him, now almost three months old, intuitively calm with my mother. He couldn't remember her, could he? Maybe it's the similarity in facial features, or tone of voice, or how we were together, but he seemed to understand that the journey was over and we were safe now with family. He smiled and cooed all day long.

That night, when I checked my e-mail on my mother's dial-up, Sarah from Kansas had written in:

God bless you for making it home.—Sarah.

CHAPTER 18

A few days later I posted an update from home:

What a weird moment in a young marriage, new
parenthood, a life. The dog is very happy
here—loves the air, the sticks, the woods, the yard,
the big family kind of thing. The baby is happy, but
his schedule is all messed up. The husband and the
wife are trying to just accept what's happened and are
almost too tired to figure a Plan B. And that's where
we are. On a lifeboat of sorts, home with family
graceful enough not to press us too much on the what
and the when of the future, enjoying small moments,
trying to rest even though the reality of what's just
happened weighs down with a force that sometimes
takes my breath away. But, and I'm counting on

this: Once green tender life begins to take over the dusty, muddy, cruddy early spring everyone endures in Maine, just the pure exuberance of nature flourishing will rekindle something somewhere within us and, I hope, bring our dreams back. Love, Caitlin, Dan, M. and Hopper.

What we realized when we arrived, and this is a hard thing to see as an adult child, was that my mother's life in the woods was becoming harder for her to maintain. Her house is not an easy place for one person to take care of. When we arrived, the roof was leaking from a huge ice dam. Wood needed to be stacked. The small pond by the house needed to be drained to the larger pond at the end of the long yard to avoid flooding from the spring rains and snowmelt, a job that required cleaning out and widening the small stream along the stone wall. A tree needed to come down. The garden needed to be planted.

Dan dove headfirst into the outdoor chores. At lunchtime he'd come in with Hopper covered in mud and sweat, his face shining from the physical labor, and he started to seem like the guy I had married: fresh-faced, strong and vibrant. He was no longer carrying the broken slump of a man who had been beaten by the world; instead, when he'd saunter in, kicking off a pair of rubber boots my mother bought him for ten dollars at Renys discount store, he looked like a man who was taking care of his family by working the land. He started to feel whole.

Inside, we were back to the *Little House on the Prairie* mode of my childhood as my mother and I sorted old seeds from the previous year and picked out seeds to order for the garden. My mother makes her living as a freelance writer. Her money was tight, too. And because it was unclear how long we would be staying, we decided to plant as much food as my mother's raised beds could handle, including carrots and pumpkins, potatoes and squashes, foods that could be harvested well into the fall. As I had in L.A., I began baking all our bread and making large pots of soup. We ordered monthly supplies of bulk foods from a neighborhood co-op and I tried to plan menus, which, as tedious as it is, does manage to help get your grocery bill down.

For a few weeks, although creditors had started dogging us and the future was uncertain, Dan and I existed in quiet stasis. What we needed more than anything was to regain our bearings. We signed up for MaineCare, the state version of Medicaid; Dan picked up odd carpentry jobs to pay for groceries; and I started working with my new agent on my book proposal. I also started learning a new angle of motherhood—motherhood from a comfortable, safe place. Even on her own turf, as she had in California, my mother gave us space to find ourselves as parents, though she was there, watching, and easily could have become bossy. This was a gift. We needed to feel this new experience was still just ours. But we did share in the joy of Matthew together with her. Often, on a warm spring morning, I'd find my mother sitting on the porch with Matthew on her lap, his little neck so tender, his head a silken tangle of blond curls. If I interrupted and asked what they were doing, she'd say, "Listening"—to the peepers, the trees, the birds—and would put her finger up to tell me to be quiet.

After everything we'd been through, being home with my mother gave us another person to talk to, another set of hands to hold our baby, another person to share the homemade food on the table—all this felt like luxury. We had been so lonely—even together—in the collapse of California. At night, Dan and I stayed up late doing dishes and tidying the house so that it was ready to be lived in in the morning (this was something we'd always done, but we'd found that with a baby, and especially with a baby in someone else's house, putting everything in order before bed was the only provision for sanity control). Sometimes, after the house was quiet and my mother and son were asleep, Dan and I would sit on the couch and spend time talking as we listened to the spring peepers make their crazy music outside and we'd eat popcorn covered with our special blend of salt and pepper, brewer's yeast and butter. Sometimes we'd play a board game like Yahtzee or Cat-Opoly—a version of Monopoly for cat lovers. I couldn't remember the last time I'd sat down and played a board game. Even when I came home for vacations there was never any time to play Uno or Mystery.

On Fridays we made homemade pizzas. I let the dough rise in the afternoon and then we'd roll it out and cover it with cheese and vegetables. It was a way to celebrate the week and do something fun together. These pizza nights were my mother's idea, and we often found ourselves laughing as we cooked and ate, and it felt good. On Saturdays we cleaned the house. We'd wash the floors and dust, change the sheets, do laundry, go to the dump. My mother liked to do the bathroom and listen to the show *Wait Wait . . . Don't Tell Me!* on public radio. Collectively we'd get the house ready for a new week. This ritualized simplicity—in a place where our cell phones didn't work and where the laptop Dan and I shared categorically rejected my mother's dial-up Internet service—put our lives in a quiet zone where we could lick our wounds and mend.

I went to the library most days of the week to check e-mail, apply for a handful of jobs and write a little on the book proposal. With my breasts full as balloons, I'd eat the lunch I'd packed with one hand and work with the other. Then I'd rush home so that Dan could take the computer and go back to the library to apply for jobs himself. For me, as a new mother, throwing as many pieces of spaghetti at the wall as possible, hoping that one might stick, had its challenges. What I wanted more than a book deal, more than a job, more than anything, was for my life to be ordered enough that I could be a stay-at-home mom. I wanted to focus on my child, to nurse and read books about babies, to maybe take a Mommy and Me class. Instead, from the moment our son was born, I had been in a full-on tussle to survive. I can imagine the mothers who tried being stay-at-home moms and hated it telling me I'm nuts, that I'm imagining a holy grail of motherhood that doesn't exist. Perhaps. But don't we always want what we can't have?

Dan and I kept wanting something to shift, for the weight of the question mark hanging over our heads to move off us. This waiting was much different from hoping. Hope can feel like a light at the end of the proverbial tunnel. The feeling that something *has* to change soon because your life has sunk too far into the unmanageable is something entirely more desperate.

But despite knowing the questions were there, hovering, in the afternoons we'd all take walks through the woods, even in the rain, with Hopper racing ahead. We decided to take the desire we cultivated in Los Angeles to understand our environment and train it on our native environment. We carried bird, tree and mammal books on our walks and tried to learn. In the built environment of the Venice canals, we'd often see a brown pelican fly overhead with a fish in its bill, coots jiving up and down the canals, a night heron fishing or a possum eating a neighbor's cat food; here, in the woods, we'd see moose tracks in wet sphagnum, coyote scat on a dirt road or a raft of buffleheads out on the water.

Some days we'd all pile into the car (even Hopper) and drive to the co-op in Blue Hill to get a cup of coffee together, our son sleeping propped in his car seat on a table as we read the paper and talked over him. Sitting there together, we were able to witness a small town and its residents firsthand. Sometimes, standing in line waiting for a veggie burrito, you'd hear a young woman ask another with total earnestness, "How are your chickens?" Not "How are your children?" Or "How is your husband?" Or even "How's your garden?" But "How are your chickens?" Once, two young mothers said goodbye to each other by bowing and saying in hushed tones, "Namaste." These things would make Dan and me laugh at the hokey hilarity of what locals might call the "back to nature on a trust fund" folks who were trying so hard to make an oasis from the world. But, also, the simplicity of their needs to sanctify their daily existence was oddly comforting.

Sometimes at the co-op or the general store, we'd run into people who had heard us on NPR. That could be nice, because the explaining of why we were home and living with my mother was already done. But often we just felt like the representative bad-luck tale from the recession. This was harder for Dan in some ways than for me, because this was my childhood community; people didn't know Dan like they knew me, so he felt one-dimensional, just a voice that had been on the radio. He felt like that Bessie Smith song, "Nobody Knows You When You're Down and Out," was written specifically for him. Every so often someone would ask why we were home, and when we gave them the condensed version, they would say, "Oh, I heard some people on NPR whose story was like that."

Some afternoons we'd drive around and look at houses for sale. This might sound crazy, but although we might never be people with enough money (or good enough credit) to own a house, we still want to believe in our dreams. When we'd gone west to California one of our hopes had been that we'd make enough money in L.A. to buy a house in Maine. We still wanted to imagine that. Once, driving around, we found a little white cape for sale, set back from the road with a long field rolling up to its rounded driveway. The house was small, but behind it was a barn and lilacs and beyond that blueberry bushes and then woods. It needed lots of work and it sagged a little under the weight of years of neglect. It reminded me of a book I'd had as a child called *The Little House* about a house that sat on a hill in the country only to one day have the city encroach and make it very sad until it got moved back out to a little hill in the country again. Our little cape sat in my mind's eye like the house in that story. The price tag was over half a million dollars, what with the acreage and woods and a view of the ocean. But here's the thing: The imagination knows no bounds, so at night, Dan and I would dream about someday having a place like that which we could fix up, and had a yard for Matthew to play in and woods for Hopper to run through. And even though that specific place was never going to happen, when we stayed up late to whisper in the dark, our son sleeping sugar-fairy dreams in my childhood bed, anything seemed possible. We just had to keep going, one foot in front of the other, one corner of the dream at a time. At the end of the day, what else do you have?

Every night at dinner, with the windows opened to the sound of spring peepers, my mother would utter the same thing, her face light and open; she'd say, "I love this evening." Sometimes in the morning, as the sun came sanding in through the screens and I sat nursing my son as Dan cooked poached eggs and homemade toast, she'd say, "I love this day." Where did this come from? I don't remember much of *that* going on as I grew up. Maybe I'd been too wrapped up in my own dramas to notice? Or maybe the turmoil of my parents' marriage had suffocated these sentiments? To my ears, saying something so hopefully lovely out loud was shocking. What I say out loud are the problems. The idea of saying that I loved a day before it even began upended my world. I thought, Who the hell is this person? I also thought, "My God, what grace that requires especially when your house has been taken over by your adult child, her husband, their ninety-pound dog and a fussing grandbaby and you have no idea when you'll get your space back." Once Dan, cautiously optimistic in my presence, said to me, "You know, maybe we should start saying that every day? It seems like a good idea? Like it might start things on a positive? No?"

"Sure," I snarled.

But he was right, she was right. If I begrudgingly tried to say "I love this day" before it began, the day started out OK. Hope said aloud, even just plain hope that you'd love the day or the evening, was buoying. And that kind of hope, the hope of affirmation, was completely different from the weight of questions, which could drive you crazy with a million what-ifs.

We didn't really have anywhere else to go, and we had no

job prospects despite our daily job applications and query letters. Still, one day, when we were out walking by the bay where we got married, Dan and I turned at exactly the same time and talking over each other said, "Let's stay here for a while."

When the garden first started coming up with a rush of lovage, a celery-like herb, we dove into cooking with the greens of spring—the lovage, the fiddleheads, the baby mustard greens and kale. Dan became obsessed with lovage. We ate it in salads and soups, underneath fish, and then he came up with a truly sublime pasta recipe, which he called Lovage or Leaf It that was full of lovage and herbs, Parmesan and cracked pepper. We often picked up shrimp from the local guys whose trucks hovered across the street from Trade Winds in Blue Hill, and I made it with an intoxicating mixture of fresh chives, rosemary and thyme, lemon, hot pepper flakes, olive oil and garlic. We'd eat the shrimp piled on top of white rice and a crisp lovage salad, and it felt like we were eating what spring might taste like if you imagined it to have a taste.

Dan began to get the odd pick-up work of carpentry and house painting. What he made wasn't yet enough to pay any big bills, but it was enough to pay for a few groceries and to start to get us back to some kind of level.

I was happy. I laughed every day. This is the wonderful thing about having a child: No matter what's going on, your child will help you see beauty and laughter everywhere. You couldn't have told me a year earlier that my life would fall apart and I'd start laughing. Maybe I'd finally learned what my brother tried to teach me. I liked seeing the spring burst into summer, I liked helping my mother with the house and garden, I liked the safety of being home and had begun to like being in the woods, where we could hide from the world. I loved seeing the things we had planted come up, tender and life-giving. I loved listening to the phoebes and robins build their nests and start their families. I didn't yet know what was being righted in my inner and outer lives by living at home with my mother, but I did know that something was healing.

CHAPTER 19

Robert Frost wrote that "nothing gold can stay." And like all good things that hit a sour patch, after about six weeks of utopia, around the exact moment when I felt like we could stay with my mother forever, things went downhill. Maybe that's how it always goes—it does in my life, anyway. I say out loud this is the best thing ever, then suddenly, it changes. In fairness we all tried very hard and, although we had been in this magical place of wonder and beauty together as a family, we are a family that still has fissures and wounds, a family of creative drives and hot tempers.

My mother, who had been, ever since Matthew's birth, so terrifically present, hit a bump. Suddenly she felt that she had no space that was hers in her own home. Undeniably, we were an extra financial strain, no matter how hard we worked to help pay for the propane, groceries, electricity and phone. It was the numbers on her bills and groceries receipts that were worrisome, less the reality of us taking on two-thirds of them, or at least promising to. For her, more people meant more of everything—more mess, more money spent, more food eaten, more noise—and less of one thing most writers need: solitude. The life she had worked hard to define as her own felt like it had been submerged in the cacophony of a small family. She became tense and remote. And then she confronted us.

I felt immediately betrayed. Where were we supposed to go? What were we supposed to do? There was, after all, only one bathroom, one small kitchen, one living room, one couch. After my mother and I exchanged a volley of angry, hurt words, Dan and I packed ourselves up in the car with our son and dog and drove off down the driveway. In the car, alone, we both broke down in tears, Dan holding the steering wheel, me in the passenger seat. We felt homeless.

For the rest of the day we drove around. It was the first hot day in May and we were overdressed and uncomfortable. We went to an Internet café in Ellsworth and I e-mailed my brother a desperate letter asking for him to call me. One of the true gifts of having a sibling can be that when you feel like your parents are impossible, your brother or sister can help you calm down and figure out what to do. This hadn't always been true with my brother and me. For years, the tensions in our family had eroded our trust in each other. But since we had both been married, something had softened between us. Maybe it was the tentative step we were both making to say yes to marriage despite the pain of our parents' divorce or maybe it was just that as we got older and as our parents did, too, not having each other was more dangerous than letting go of our past. My brother called me and listened. He was able to understand everyone from all sides, which is a talent of his. He offered the sobering wisdom that we needed to make this living arrangement with my mother work because we might need to be there for quite a bit longer. The question, he said, was how to preserve our dignity and also forgive wholeheartedly, which we must do.

After I got off the phone, Dan and I went to the health-food store and ate some hummus and pretzels for lunch because that was all we could afford. We drank glasses of free water. Then we drove to my father's, hungry and tired. He made us ice water with lemon, gave us some sandwiches and sat with us in his airy living room and told us to go back, try again, make it OK. Dan asked my dad if he could give us an advance on the bookshelves Dan had already begun making for him, so that we might now pay my mom some of the promised debt for bills and also pay ahead a little bit to alleviate some financial anxiety.

We got back into the car knowing that no matter how beat-up we felt, we needed to keep things steady for our son. We just needed to work this out.

On the way home, we deposited the check and got out some cash. When we pulled into the driveway it was evening and my mother's car was gone. She had left a note that read:

"I've gone to a meeting and will be back later. Please stay. I'm sorry."

We made ourselves food, cleaned our dishes and retreated to our two small rooms at the back of her house. We left the cash on the counter with an itemized note of what it would cover that we owed her and got ready for an early bedtime.

In the morning we made a wary, bruised truce. I knew I had to forgive. I had my son to think about and our stability. My husband had been emasculated to the point where he felt everything he did was witnessed by my parents and their friends. He felt exposed as he scrambled for house-painting, fix-it-man and lawn-maintenance jobs. And I had come home with a husband, a child and nowhere else to go. We felt like failures. But—and this may be the hardest point of a lesson that I needed to learn—it was when I felt like I had nothing that I could gain something. I didn't know this yet; I was too wrapped up in feeling frightened and angry. But in taking a big gulp and realizing that this was my mother's house and that, for our own survival, we had to forgive and go on, we were forcibly choosing family. More than that, I was choosing to love my mother.

Mom and I were distant for a few days. During that time, Dan planned afternoons when he would drop me off at the library and then go with our son to my father's for the day, letting my father and stepmother babysit while he worked on the shelves to make the money we'd already been given or searched for jobs on my dad's computer. The idea was to take as much time and space away as we needed so that my mother and I could calm down.

As we stepped outside of our routine enough to spend long hours with my dad, I was glad to see him take time away from his work to lie on a blanket with Matthew and play. His tenderness with my young son touched me at the core. I might never have seen this if we had not gone home.

Spring gave way to summer and the garden went into full, luxurious production. Lawns were being mowed, and as we passed through Blue Hill going back and forth from my mother's to the library and on to my father's, we opened all the windows to let in the mix of salt air and mown grass. I started walking long distances when Dan was working odd jobs, pushing the stroller as I tried to take off some of my post-baby bulge. Lilacs bloomed everywhere and I gathered big bunches of them to fill my mother's house. She allowed us to invite our friends Tim and Jess for Memorial Day weekend and helped us clean the house for their arrival. We put lilacs in every room and made them a bed on a blow-up mattress in my old room. They arrived, Jess as stylishly homespun as ever, a big wooden picnic basket over her arm filled with a homemade rhubarb pie and local cheeses, wine and beer. We spent a wonderful few days together, my mother as much a part of the weekend as we were. It was then that I understood why I needed to get back to a place of love and not retreat into anger. Not just because we had nowhere to go—although that was a point of soreness that hit every abandonment nerve inside me—but because I knew that the future of my emotional life depended on coming back to a place of warmth. We all needed this to be a success, not a failure.

The morning after Tim and Jess left, I made up my mind to give my mother a hug and thank her for having our friends visit and for having us there. We were guests again, I felt. Something had felt ruptured to the point where we weren't necessarily a multigenerational commune working together on an equal playing field for the greater common good. But as guests, we were safe and could, maybe, in time make ourselves at home once more.

Like that, we were over the mountain. A lightness came back to our dinners as the long evening light waned, the windows gushed in fragrant summer smells and our son jumped like a maniac in his Jumperoo.

CHAPTER 20

With no real luck on the job front, Dan and I started to feel that we needed to man up, as I like to say (which drives Dan nuts), and approach everything with a new spin. With record numbers of unemployed and homeless in America and with collapse after collapse of industry after industry despite predictions that things would be (and some even dared say, were) picking up, we were unsure what exactly we should be manning up to do.

In early May, Dan accepted a position teaching a summer class at an art school in Portland, a three-hour drive down the coast. This presented both a logistical challenge and a financial one. And although taking any kind of risk felt entirely stupid, we thought, OK, someone's career has to go somewhere. Let's roll the dice here and go for this class that will bring in a minuscule amount of cash but get Dan teaching again and also get us to Portland on a weekly basis to look for other work. An incredibly kind couple, whose own children had married and left home and who owned a large brick townhouse in Portland with an empty third floor for guests, offered us refuge any night we wanted it. They gave us a key.

I will never forget the sheer amount of time spent that summer in the car with our baby, our dog and what seemed like a small mountain of gear (why doesn't it matter with a baby if you're going for one night or one season, driving to Portland or across America, you lug the same amount of stuff?) shuttling back and forth the three hours from downeast Maine to Portland. In every visit we'd accomplish job hunting, Dan's teaching and a recording session or an interview for a radio piece; then we'd return to my mother's for three or four days where we sent e-mails and résumés and where I stole a few hours to work on my book proposal and send a few more pitches to public radio. Dan squeezed in a few extra handy-man jobs for summer people arriving in Blue Hill. Then we'd pile back into the car to go down to Portland to apply for and interview for more jobs and Dan would teach again. From the car we made phone calls to anyone and everyone we thought might have job leads, job ideas, magazine or menial work—anything we could think of. Matty was not quite six months old and was still nursing all the time, so we stopped to nurse on the side of the road. We started his first solid foods on the road without a high chair; we continued to change diapers in our laps.

We came up with a song to sing to Matty that went like this: "*Old MacDonald lived in his car, eee-I—ee—I—O. And in that car he had a dog, ee-I—ee—I—O. With a ruff ruff here and a ruff ruff there . . .*" A couple of times Dan booked photo jobs that took him out of town for a few nights and I'd stay at our friends' home, alone with the baby and the dog. I was often lonely. I missed our friends' noises and presence in their own home. I missed Dan. I missed my mother. I thought maybe we'd always be living this way and never have a place of our own.

I often found myself thinking about Moses in the bulrushes as I watched Matthew wake up in his car seat or on the bed at our friends' townhouse, his little eyes confused, his mouth opening into the perfect square of a cry as he tried to figure out where he was. I hoped that when he saw my face that would be enough. The one thing we made sure of, as arbitrary as this seems, was that our baby and I took a bath together every day at six p.m., no matter what was happening, no matter where we were. We hung on to this schedule for dear life. What we could not give our child in a predictable environment, we tried to give him in baths.

When Dan was with us in Portland, by night in the guest room we opened mail, figured out what bills could be paid, strategized and argued. And by day, Dan walked up and down the streets, going into bars and restaurants to apply for jobs. Sometimes there'd be an opening posted in the paper or someone would tell us that a bartender was needed. Dan is a very good bartender and has an impeccable reputation for being so in Portland. On and off in Los Angeles, before the economy went south, Dan had bartended for catering companies and private parties. But that summer in Maine, at place after place, there were hundreds of applicants in line for each job. Even in a small city like Portland, whose population is little more than 60,000, with the surrounding metro area totaling closer to 500,000, notices for bartenders were receiving record numbers of applicants. Once, Dan turned to me and said, "Anyone who thinks this thing is over with is deluded or such an insulated asshole they have no credibility with me." He applied for a custodial job for the city of Portland, a job doing school pictures for a set of mid-coast schools, and put in bids for roofing and carpentry jobs. Everywhere, he was in a queue of hundreds. Then something happened.

I remember the day perfectly. It was raining and it was morning. We were in Portland and Dan was about to go out from the safety of our friends' townhouse to hit the pavement again. I was nursing Matthew, and outside the green leaves of the trees shook in the wind and rain. Dan's cell phone rang. It was someone from a local Maine food company with a national reputation that had its own in-house photography department and was looking for a new head photographer. The photographer who was leaving knew of Dan's work and had heard we were home and that Dan needed a job. He wondered when Dan could come in to meet the owners and do a test shoot. Dan asked, "Tomorrow?" He said yes.

Luckily, we had packed Dan a collared shirt and a nice pair of pants. And although he was a little ragtag, needing a haircut and his skin still broken out from stress, after a nice hot shower and with a clean pressed shirt on, he looked great.

He went in and shot a bunch of blueberries, lemons, colanders and bread on a marble countertop. When he came back there was a spring in his step and I could tell he felt great. He told me he'd hit the ball out of the park. He was sure he'd gotten it. I need to qualify this because if you don't already know this about Dan, he is not an arrogant guy. He doesn't usually think that he's hit any balls out of any park, and especially at this time in our lives when we felt so downtrodden, this was not a natural reaction for him. But he knows his stuff. He knows how to light things and make even the most pedestrian blueberry look like it's going to tea with the Queen of England. Our lives were about to turn around. I could feel it. This job had good benefits and a great salary. We might, in just a few short weeks, be on the road to some kind of recovery. It was June and Dan hadn't been working steadily for nearly six months. This was our break.

Monday came and we went home to my mother's. No call came that day. That evening Dan turned to me and said, "That's funny. They said they'd make a decision by the end of the day Friday or, latest, Monday."

"It's fine," I said. "They're trying to figure out the money or something."

My mother, also, told Dan, "I'm sure they're just figuring out a package." My mother has a way of dispensing information in such a definitive way that you don't question it. When my brother and I were younger, she taught us to say (as a joke, I promise) "My mother is always right," and we'd often sass her with that refrain. So, what with my mother endorsing the silence and me making it seem logical, we were all so sure. When he had left on Friday one of the owners had suggested a nice town for us to live in south of Portland and closer to their headquarters. Dan's photos had been spot on. His references were stellar.

Tuesday came. No call. Then Wednesday came and went. By Thursday, after a night of no sleep in the loft bedroom by himself, Dan had decided that he would call them. Waiting to hear from this potential employer, Dan had reached a new level of anxiety and embarrassment that was almost impossible to bear. His voice had gotten quiet again and his shoulders slumped. He felt ashamed in front of my parents. This was all playing out so publicly, how could he not? That morning he walked outside while I nursed Matty. He stood a little ways away from the porch on the lawn and called the woman to whom he would directly report. He left her a voice mail. And then, just as we were piling into the car to go to my dad's to have lunch, his cell rang. He got out of the car and walked to a small outcrop of trees while Matty, Hoppy and I waited. He got back in the car and said nothing.

"So?" I asked.

"That was MassArt. They're offering me one of their eight spots for the fall."

"What?"

"I just got into graduate school, Caitlin."

"Holy fucking shit. What? Oh my God!" I got out and yelled to my mother in the house. She opened a window and yelled out, "See, Dan, something's going to work out! That's amazing! I'm so happy for you!"

This was a success Dan needed more than anything at that moment. I'm sure I also don't need to tell you that this was followed by a silence in the car that invited the question, How in the world can we ever pay for graduate school? My heart felt squeezed because I knew that this was Dan's dream: He had always wanted to teach and he'd always wanted the extra push a prestigious graduate program would give his career.

I wanted to do anything to make it happen for him. I, myself, had spent two years applying to the top MFA acting programs in the country. I was flat-out rejected. Once, in an information session after our auditions, the head of a top program told a room of fifty white women that there were, at best, only two spots for white women in their upcoming class of six and that, by and large, this applicant group was the largest. I was thirty and, although I looked younger than I was, I was a confusing candidate for these programs: I already had my own theater company, I had a freelance career with public radio, I was a published writer and yet . . . I wanted to be an actress? I did. I love acting. This is paradoxical because it's certainly the métier I've excelled at the least and received the smallest amount of accolades for. But I love the way you can take an emotion and sift it through your body like the finest sugar until you know with conviction that even your toes understand how your character feels. I love how afterward, if you've done your job right, although exhausted, you've really let something go inside you. I love that when acting is true and from the heart, I believe it is the most vulnerable art form there is and also the bravest. I love being someone other than myself. The world, however, had other plans for me and I wasn't up for trying this over and over year after year. I know actors who have done that and, after six years and a fortieth birthday, they finally get into Yale. But I didn't have the money or the foolhardy patience to try time and time again. For me, the perfect place to be was radio; it's a symbiotic hybrid of writing and acting, voice and emotion. Although I don't always get the same release with radio work as I did from acting, when I am putting a radio piece together from raw sound, I often feel like I'm trying to hold a slippery, live fish. And this is exhilarating.

When we went to California, I still had this lingering hope that I might rekindle my acting career, even though, by then, I was thirty-three. Pregnancy slowed that plan down. But just after we had our child, I was filled with the deep desire to act again. I had wells of emotional information I hadn't known existed before I gave birth. Everything felt deeper, more important, more imperative. I hoped to lose my baby weight and put myself back out there. But then, everything fell apart. My acting dream wasn't even on life support by the time we left L.A.

In the car that day in Maine when Dan got into graduate school, I was quiet as my mind shuttered through all the dreams I'd had that had been killed in the last year and all the dreams I'd ever had in my whole life and how far away so many of them felt. We had a child to whom we were devoted and needed to care for the best we could, no matter what that meant. And yet. Here it was: A dream had arrived in a package with a bow even though we were in an unfortunate place from which to accept it. Either direction my mind went panicked me: What if this was the only thing that panned out? What then? How could this be a smart—scratch that—*responsible* thing to do? I kept thinking, "I hope to God this job comes through, because at least that will give us a choice we can intelligently make. Options. I want options." When we got to my dad's, he put hot dogs and buns on his picnic table on the porch and Gail put out salad, her own bread and butter pickles and ice water with lemon slices.

As we sat down to eat, Dan's cell phone rang. It was the head of Human Resources at the job calling to say she was sorry but they'd gone with another applicant. Dan had never met this Human Resources person, and she had no information on why. Dan crumpled. This was the one thing he'd thought would save us. Here we were in limbo once again. And we'd been so foolishly sure.

"How could this happen?!" I wanted to scream. *"Is the universe mocking us?"* Wildly I looked around and saw nothing to beat up

except my hot dog with mustard and pickles, so I sat down, slumped, and ate. I put my hand on Dan's knee, letting him know I was right there with him. Even so, ours was a gloomy, silent lunch. Afterward Dan got up, washed his plate and mine and went down to the basement to work on my dad's shelves. I nursed Matty and lay down with him for a nap.

That night Dan told me that the hardest thing about this would be telling his son that he couldn't go to school and follow his dreams. He wanted our lives, he said, more than anything, to be an example of dream-following, not the opposite. But, he said, he knew that this was next to impossible. We'd need a miracle. Despite the fact that he was given loans to cover the whole thing, we had no steady income and no jobs were working out.

Luckily, MassArt said they could wait for a decision for a month. In that month we called everyone we could think of once again and applied for every job we found online in the Boston/New England/Southern Maine areas. During each trip to Portland we looked at apartments because we figured Maine was cheaper than Boston by about a grand a month in living expenses, even including Dan's travel two hours each way by bus on the days he had class. We started hatching a tentative plan that revolved around the idea that if Dan could get some kind of bartending job that brought in at least $600 a week and if I could work for my theater company at $600 a month plus file one radio piece a month, then possibly we could, very tightly, make it so that Dan could go to school. The problem lay in finding Dan the bartending job during a major recession and in my realistically being able to find the time to do the work for my theater company, plus the radio pitching and producing, and also, somehow, take care of Matthew.

In late June we set ourselves up at my mother's for the long haul. It just felt wise to hunker down. We rearranged our rooms at the back of Mom's house and figured out a way to put a mattress on the floor so that we could all sleep together (as long as Dan and I were willing to let one shoulder blade each hang off the bed). Such a snug loveliness came to our two rooms with the nice beige rug on the floor in the library, the sunlight hitting it in deep pools and in the smaller back room our bed made neatly each day. Above, in the loft, where Dan had slept, we stored our clothes and laid out our bills and paperwork. As I was tidily arranging our things I remember thinking, Gosh, we don't really need that much room, do we? Each time Ma and Pa moved their family, Ma would make their simple things—often in dugout houses or bare wooden cabins—clean and bright and homey for her family. This was a lesson I learned rereading those books as an adult: Make it neat and add something pretty, even a couple of daisies in a Ball jar, because it will make a world of difference.

We felt reunited as a family on our mattress on the floor. At night Dan and I would climb into bed next to our son's sleeping body and we'd whisper in the dark everything we wanted and hoped for, everything we were grateful for, all the things that made us scared. There was an intimacy to these nightly confessions, our son breathing between us, his little body still young enough to be oblivious to our noises as he slept, our hearts still open and vulnerable despite the fear that could hold them.

In late July, my mother bought us both haircuts for fifteen dollars each because she felt that we needed some sprucing up. If we felt better about ourselves, she argued, we'd present more successfully to the world. I must admit that new haircuts, despite being just simple trims, did put an extra spring in both our steps. As the earth around us transformed into full, verdant summer mode, we, too, took some cues from nature and tried to enjoy ourselves. Every so often we went out for an ice cream at the homemade ice cream shack in Blue Hill or got a clam roll at the Fish Net. We'd count the change in our wallets to pay for one ice cream to share, or one clam roll. On the Fourth of July we cleaned my mother's house from top to bottom and invited all her neighbors over for a community potluck. We felt we must somehow participate in summer with all its loveliness because joy could be fleeting.

Then, out of nowhere, our friend Sam, a well-known chef, called and said he knew of a couple of restaurants in Brunswick, thirty minutes north of Portland, that were opening and looking for bartenders. He said that Dan could use his name.

So, the last week of July, Dan went down to Portland one last time. He met with the chefs of three restaurants in Brunswick and saw a handful of apartments. He taught his class. He spent the night at our friends' townhouse and then, the next morning, his phone rang. He was offered two bartending jobs. He called me, ecstatic. I said, "Call MassArt, honey. Let's go for this." That same day he took an apartment for us on the third floor of a Victorian building that looked out over the roofs of Portland to the sea on one side and downtown on the other. When he came home to my mother's, he looked like a new man. I remember regarding him over breakfast the next morning and thinking, My God, all it takes is a job! He's sitting taller, his skin already looks better. Man, and by man I mean all of us, wants to work. We want to contribute to our lives, our families, our communities. When good people are robbed of this opportunity, it breaks their spirits.

My mother was overjoyed that we were gunning for Dan's MFA. She, all along, was insistent that we try, as a family, to find a way for Dan to go to graduate school. She kept saying, "This is a way to the future for you guys. This is Dan's dream. You have to do this. We can make this happen, I know we can." She had been helping us think about how to get our costs as low as possible and had even gone out on a limb and sent out an e-mail to family asking for whatever financial help they could give. "This is possible," she kept saying. "I really believe it is."

With Dan's two bartending jobs and three days of classes in Boston and the pressure on me to work during Matty's naps and at night while he slept, I knew we were going to be spread thin. But it was going to be worth it. This was the break we had been waiting for.

CHAPTER 21

O n the first of August we had an apartment to go to in a few days, my thirty-fifth birthday to celebrate, school to get ready for, and for Dan, a job to begin. Although I'd be lying if I told you I felt like everything was going to work out perfectly, there was an upswing to our spirits. At night, I fretted: "Dan, how is this going to go with one car and you commuting to work three nights and then gone three days a week—how am I going to take care of Matthew and also make the money I need to make? What if none of this pans out? Are you sure this is going to be enough money? What if it fails?" I'm always like this. And Dan is always like this: "It's a start, Cait. Having a job makes it easier to get a better job, closer to Portland so I won't need the car. Maybe one day a week one of your parents can come down to watch Matty so you can do your work. And I can always drop out if it's not working." The rock was that, of course, with another degree it was possible our futures would get better. The hard place was getting there.

I wrote on my blog:

> By the end of the weekend we will have unloaded all
> our things from the U-Haul storage unit into our new
> apartment. The one glaringly obvious absence will be
> Ellison, whose bed I worry about seeing in the sad
> pile of our stuff. Somehow I keep thinking that when
> we pull all of our belongings out of that ten by ten
> steel cage, she will be there, too. This and many more
> scars from this last year and a half of our lives will
> come with us into this brave new start.

One morning when I was particularly anxious and Dan was inside feeding Matthew puréed prunes and bananas, I sat on the front step of my mother's porch with a cup of decaf coffee and my mother came out and sat down beside me, our bare feet almost touching on the cool ground below. Her feet are wide and sturdy, strong and capable-looking. Mine taper at the heel (a shape that makes my shoes almost always slip off) and my feet are a full size and a half smaller than hers. Also my ankles slope inward, a feature that looks slightly weak. There was a time when I was younger that I feigned embarrassment by my mother's big, durable feet, especially when they were stuck in a pair of Birkenstocks (which my high school gym teacher used to call "cow patties"). How nice it would have been, I imagined, to have a mother wearing nice little calfskin flats like the ones I saw in *Vogue* or *Glamour.* The truth for me was more complicated than embarrassment: When I look at my mother's feet, I feel safe. I can't explain it. Her feet are never cold like mine always seem to be. And when she rests them on the earth, as she had this morning while we sat side by side together, they look so—there's no other way to say it— *grounded.* Her hands, also, make me feel that the world can be molded to fit what I need. They're stocky and strong—even now with the onset of arthritis—and she can lift anything and fix most things. This is partly the nature of her extremities, but also a certain determination of spirit that does not fade with illness or age. I've got long, willowy hands, and I have a hard time opening anything. I hate my hands to be cold or uncomfortable. When you stop to think about it, if you're asked to describe your mother's hands or feet, you get very deeply into your story with her, don't you? It's not a usual question, yet those two places on the body tell almost more than the voice or eyes.

Anyway, on that morning, as my mother and I sat next to each other, we were listening to the hummingbirds' wings whirr in the air around us as they flitted in and out of the honeysuckle that grows up the porch. I was thinking about the amount of time our lives had felt like they were dangling over some precipice. I was thinking about how far Dan and I had come in just five short months. I was also thinking about this leap out onto our own and how, even at thirty-five years old with a husband and a baby, it felt scary to leave my mother's home. Maybe scarier than ever. So much was at stake now.

After a while, my mother said, "You can always come back, Cait," like she knew what I was thinking. "I will always take you back and, you know, we had a rough spot for a little while there, but this has been wonderful for me. And I'll miss you. I think we did beautifully at this—better than any other family I can imagine. And if you have to come back, we'll do it again. Don't worry. You're not out in L.A. with nowhere to go, you're only in Portland. You can come home. I'm your safety net."

I felt this lump rise in my throat because this, maybe, was what I'd been yearning for my mother to say to me ever since my parents' divorce, and maybe earlier. Until this moment, I'd felt, all my adult life, that I was swinging in the breeze without a tether. I had spent most of my time finding reasons— boyfriends, work, dramas—to not come home. Sitting there, my thin right foot touching the rougher side of my mother's left, it occurred to me that the whole reason I'd come home was to finish this piece of business: I needed her to tell me that she was my safety net, that I could come home again. I needed this so that I could go back out into the world. I took a deep breath and murmured, "Thank you." There was so much more I wanted to say, but I didn't know where to begin. Instead, I put my head down on my mother's shoulder, my coffee cup cradled in my lap, and closed my eyes.

Over the next few days Dan went back and forth to our new apartment and painted our bedroom a lovely blue hyacinth color that made me feel like we should be sitting down to crumpets and clotted cream on our bed and he painted Matthew's room a pale cornflower blue. He painted our new doorless nook that would be our "office" a clean white and our dining room a creamy ivory. He moved our things, once again, from the storage unit into our apartment. Then he came back to my mother's and we celebrated my birthday with a chocolate cake with chocolate frosting my mother had made from a recipe she used for Aran's and my birthdays when we were kids; she had decorated the cake with orange and gold nasturtium blossoms.

In those final days we had a memorial service for Ellison. We planted a white lilac on my mother's front lawn in Ellison's honor, sprinkling some of her ashes into its white, delicate roots. We played Greg Brown's song "Two Little Feet" on a small boombox. It was hot and sunny and my mother held Matthew in just a diaper, an umbrella shading his peachy skin. I read the St. Francis Prayer aloud and we all observed a moment of tentative silence.

Then we packed up. It was with a heavy heart that I saw how quickly our little place in the world that had felt simple and good was gone and we were back out on our own. It's not that I wasn't excited to be alone with my family, but I remarked on how easily my mother's house went back to its recognizable shape, without even the smallest trace that we had spent five months making it our home, too.

That night, we had a feast to celebrate everything that had happened and everything that was coming. My mother bought lobsters from our fisherman friend down the road and we drank a bottle of wine Dan and I had been given as a wedding present two years earlier and had been saving for a suitably perfect occasion. We ate salad from the garden and crusty bread from a local bakery run by young hipster musicians who were making some of the most sublime bread around and we finished it all off with a cherry crisp and homemade frozen yogurt with cardamom, cinnamon, lemon peel and vanilla. After dinner we sang songs to Matthew as I rocked him on my lap. When he was unwilling to go to bed, we pulled out some CDs and danced, in the living room, letting our bodies go loose and free, the three of us passing Matthew between us, Hopper jumping excitedly at our feet.

Once, in the dark, I walked outside with Hopper so that he could pee. The light from the house fell like golden puddles on the green lawn and I could hear the music and laughter inside from my mother, Dan and our infant son. I looked around at the familiar trees and the earth that had so gently taken us back when we needed the balm of nature to soothe our wounds. The woods stood around me now, absorbing our celebration, sentry to our small flicker of joy in the wilderness. I felt safe, finally.

Later, my mother and Hopper and I went out for a swim in the dark. A spring tide had made the ocean wide and deep, and the moon glinted off the almost black water. We splashed around and then, refreshed, went home to bed. I had never gone night swimming with my mother. Actually, I don't recall ever going night swimming, which is probably odd for a kid who grew up on the coast of Maine. Swimming with my mother that night was almost like a rite of some kind. Anyway, it was one of the high points of my life.

The next morning, our car filled once again with our worldly possessions, our son, our dog and a little wooden box of what remained of Ellison's ashes in the front console, we said goodbye to my mother and drove down the driveway, the trees whispering windy goodbyes.

EPILOGUE; OR, WHAT HAPPENS TO A DREAM DEFERRED?

Dearest Reader,

I sold my book. But you already know that. The day my agent called to tell me, we had sixteen dollars in our bank account and an empty fridge. Things had gotten harder because business in the restaurants where Dan was bartending was slack and he wasn't bringing in half of what we needed. I was taking care of Matty during the day and working late into the night on freelance work. Because of the sheer strain, Dan was considering dropping out of school. On that day, even though it was the end of September, it was still warm enough to swim. When my cell phone rang, Matthew and Hopper and I were at the beach, rolling around in the late-afternoon water, which glinted as if flecked with solid bits of sunshine. I sat down on the sand and almost fainted. Our lives, in one afternoon, changed. Some air was let in.

So, does this story end like Cinderella with a happily ever after and a flourish? Not really. Lives are lived on a continuum. Even now, more than a year after we've come home, I sometimes feel pangs of shame that all we have to show for our time out west is nothing but a huge pile of bills. I still feel remorse for everything that could have been in Los Angeles. I still make lists of all the things I never did or saw in L.A. because I was too sick or we were too broke: Disney Concert Hall, Lucques restaurant, the Rose Bowl Flea Market, the L.A. County Fair, Joshua Tree, the Santa Monica Public Library. I miss the friends I made in L.A., who were bright, kind and exciting people to share my life with. And as I write this, our country is still in a devastatingly hard place.

Does this story end, then, with a lesson? Maybe. We are a family just like yours in many ways, a family that works hard, tries to eat well, attempts to make the best decisions for the children and is learning to be flexible with the ebbs and flows of life. As of this writing, Dan is still in school working on his master's, and when he's not doing that or being a father, he's working for commercial clients or doing odd jobs. I'm still trying to keep a freelance career afloat. Slowly, with the help of my book advance, we're bailing out from the financial avalanche of lives that fell apart. And we're also trying to do what lots of young couples do—have a marriage and raise a child, two things that often seem at odds. We're still trying to achieve our dreams, though for a time there we thought dreaming was either plain dumb or dangerous.

What we learned from our lives going belly-up was to simplify. There's a difference, it turns out, between following your dreams and getting your life in so much debt you get crushed when a crisis hits. This is the American problem. Somewhere in the disastrous melding of the inflation of costs—food, homes, goods—and the necessity to buy, buy, buy, we all lost sight of what we really needed. Greg Brown says in a song "We have no knowledge and so we have stuff and stuff with no knowledge is never enough." He's right; this is true. Dan and I learned in a short period of time that getting a land line with no features, cutting cell phone plans back to nothing, making bread and granola each week and trying to buy as much of our food from local farmers as possible would not only keep us but save us. We learned that someday, if we ever have a house and a little piece of earth, we want to grow our own vegetables, raise our own chickens for eggs. We won't forget, because it truly is a gift to be simple.

But there's something more, the reason I've taken all these pages to tell you this story: What was much harder for me to learn than the many ways a simpler life can sustain me was that the bonds of family will sometimes support me more than my career. Ambitions, although wonderful, keep my mind out of the present and always on the future; they let me dream that "one fine morning . . ." When hanging together as a family became bigger than just "important" and our survival really depended on it, I learned I could live in the fine mornings of my present rather than strive constantly ahead. We need each other. I need my family, I need my friends, I need my communities (neighbors, colleagues, fellow writers, strangers who might listen to me on the radio). And these days I think that until all Americans realize this—how much we need each other—that some of us will always be falling through the cracks, every single moment of every single day.

At the end of October, when the air was still warm and sunny, Dan and I piled ourselves and Matty and Hopper into the car to go apple picking. In the six years we'd been together, we had never gone apple picking, despite living most of that time in a state famous for its apples and even though my mother used to take my brother and me, every fall, so that we could store up a winter's supply in our root cellar. Why now? We went because we had a child whom we wanted to experience being outside in a orchard on a lovely fall day, but also because of everything we felt we'd lost; we no longer wanted to miss anything. And we, too, wanted to stock up for the winter.

The orchard was empty. We let Hopper run and dodge between the trees and we began picking Jonagolds and Cortlands, Galas and Empires. The sun poured, golden and thick, like shafts of waxy wildflower honey through the trees, making Matty's hair shine and our skin glow. We tasted variety after variety, our stomachs bursting with their sweet, juicy, fibrous flesh as crows danced in the trees next to us, cackling at us as we celebrated a bacchanal of apples. Our son, then ten months old, held out his fat, gummy hand and picked, with surprising agility, his first apple, then clutched it like a prize. I remember thinking, with the endless blue sky above, the light, the color and smell of apples and earth and trees and fall, the mountains and valleys in the distance, that I was finally at peace. My life had come back to a kind of order. I knew who I was, where I was meant to be. It was here in this place, with my small, brave family, that I found some kind of Eden. We had gone all the way to the land of milk and honey only to come home to this garden of abundance, this place made, it seemed, just for us.

As we drove home, I put my head on Dan's square shoulder, his warmth coming through his sweatshirt and caressing my cheek. Then I reached back to hold my son's hand as he began to doze, having tired of his apple. Hopper, somehow, managed to rest his head on my arm and he closed his eyes with a deeply satisfied groan. Totally connected, meaty flesh to meaty flesh, with our haul of apples in the back of the car, our day came to a close. On the radio Lyle Lovett's voice flooded the dusky light, the sun peeling away from the sides of the road as we drove:

> *If you needed me*
> *I would come to you*
> *I'd swim the seas*
> *For to ease your pain.*

This Land Was Made for You and Me

This land is your land, this land is my land
From California to the New York Island
From the Redwood Forest to the Gulf Stream waters
This land was made for you and me.

As I went walking that ribbon of highway
And saw above me that endless skyway
And saw below me the golden valley, I said:
This land was made for you and me.

I roamed and rambled and followed my footsteps
To the sparkling sands of her diamond deserts
And all around me, a voice was sounding:
This land was made for you and me.

Was a big high wall there that tried to stop me
A sign was painted said: Private Property
But the back side, it didn't say nothing—
That side was made for you and me.

When the sun came shining, then I was strolling
In wheat fields waving, and dust clouds rolling
The voice was chanting as the fog was lifting:
This land was made for you and me.

One bright sunny morning, in the shadow of a steeple;
By the relief office, I saw my people—
As they stood there hungry, I stood there wonderin' if
This land was made for you and me?

Matty and Hopper, in a hotel on the long road home, April 2009.

My mother's saltbox in the woods, Downeast Maine, summer 2009.

ACKNOWLEDGMENTS

Every once in a while a dream gets made. Rarely does this happen with just one person toiling away; more often than not it takes a village. In *my* case, it took something more like a small city.

When Kate Lee and I first spoke, I knew I had gotten really lucky. She's everything anyone wants in a dream agent: smart, opinionated, thoughtful, ballsy. When the proposal for this book was ready, she went to Barbara Jones at Voice. Barbara got everything—my story, the way I write, what I wanted to say to a larger audience, what my dreams were, what scared me. Six months later, Barbara took an unwieldy first draft and helped me shape my first book. Without her thoughtful changes both big and small, without her just being on the other end of the line, this book could never have been written.

When anyone ever asks me about Voice, I say the same thing: I've died and gone to heaven. From Ellen Archer, the president of Hyperion Books and Voice, to Betsy Wilson, Claire McKean, Laura Klynstra, Allison McGeehon and everyone who has helped make this book and then sell it, I cannot write enough praise.

And then there are the friends who cheered us on as we traveled back and forth across the country, as we put our lives back together: Craig Pospisil; Vanessa Moore; Frank Menair; Anne and Darren Hendler; Andrea Meyer and Harlan Bosmajian; Annette Lemieux and Erik Hansen; Terry Tempest Williams; Libbet Cone; Anne Esguerra and Corey Koch; Jordan Scott; John Saldana; Joan and Daniel Amory; Sam Hayward; Kathleen Bender; Guy Miracle and Lance Castro. Frank Williams was our angel more than once. On our long road home, Jessica and Tim Rhys wrote to me: "Tell Dan we will organize a parade for him this summer . . . or at least buy him a lobster." Well, they came through on the lobster.

Then there were the people who made our lives better, even though they didn't have to: Annette and Rob Elowitch gave me a room on the top floor of their beautiful home in which to write this book; Sandra Richardson and Leah Whalen were faithful readers; Peter Davis made a suggestion of how to tell this story that was invaluable; Rob McCall offered us faith and guidance; David Ghozland not only delivered our son but also became our friend; Dr. Carlsen escorted Ellison, Dan and me through Ellison's death; Sarah Willits and all the readers of my blog who wrote in and kept us going; Greg Brown for his music both ways across the country and then his generosity in letting me reprint some of it here.

To these amazing people at NPR: Scott Simon, Tom Cole, Walter Watson, Rolando Arrieta and, especially, Andrea de Leon. If she had not commissioned my series of audio diaries, I would never have known how many people were touched by circumstances like mine.

Thank you to my family. Specifically, to my mother, Susan Hand Shetterly, who took us in and sent us back out into the world more whole, and to my father, Robert Shetterly, and his partner, Gail Page, who helped and cared for us more than could be told in this book. To Cherie and Ken Mason, and also to the memories of Grammar and Trav, Birdie and Pop.

Thank you to Ellison and Hopper, who went west with Dan and me, and to our son, who came east with us when he was two months old and has gamely embraced our lives as an adventure.

And, finally, to Dan, who read each and every draft of this book, who cheered me on and made me tea; who was right by my side through not only the worst but also the best of tough times, and who, at the end of every day, said "I love you, goodnight."

PERMISSIONS